Catch
CARP AND TENCH

D1016147

JOHN WILSON

BOXTREE

Catch
CARP

This edition published 2001 by Boxtree
an imprint of Pan Macmillan Ltd
Pan Macmillan, 20 New Wharf Road,
London N1 9RR
Basingstoke and Oxford
Associated companies throughout the world
www.panmacmillan.com

ISBN 978-0-7522-1926-4

Originally published as *Catch Carp with John Wilson* 1991 by Boxtree
and *Catch Tench with John Wilson* 1991 by Boxtree

Illustrations by David Batten
Printed and bound in Great Britain by CPI Bath

CONTENTS

ACKNOWLEDGEMENTS

No angling writer can produce a book without considerable help from others. Allow me therefore to thank the editing and design team, the mates who leave their own fishing to photograph me, and a very special thank you to good friend Dave Batten who has made such a fine job of the line drawings.

John Wilson
Great Witchingham
1991

INTRODUCTION

ONLY 35 years ago, back in the mid 1950s, most anglers simply talked about the mystique surrounding carp, few actually ever saw the fish in their landing-net. Today the situation has been completely reversed as more and more fisheries become stocked with this exciting species. Carp are now the most sought after freshwater fish in Britain, surpassing in popularity even the roach. The reasons for this are not difficult to understand. Carp quickly grow to a large size, providing everyone with their best chance of coming to grips with a fish of 10 lb and more. They fight harder than all other species found in both still and running water, with the exception of perhaps salmon and catfish. And they are not difficult to catch when stocked in reasonable numbers. What is more, being a durable, long-living creature they are the 'perfect' stock fish guaranteed to provide fishery owners with value for money and anglers with a powerful adversary whether it weighs 3 lb or 30 lb. And this surely is the carp's real strength. Whatever its size, it provides a thrilling battle.

This book is about my ways of catching carp and subsequently enjoying catching carp of all sizes. It is not a manual for those interested only in monster specimens, which require much dedication and a single-minded approach. I make no secret of the fact that I have yet to find enough time to pursue this goal. To many, carp fishing is about putting up a bivi for the weekend, casting out a couple of ledgered baits and sitting back waiting for runs to develop. It is not my idea of carp fishing. I simply haven't the time. My carp are invariably caught during short pre-work sessions or perhaps in the evening as the light starts to go, and occasionally at midday. I simply enjoy the never-ending challenge of catching carp of different colours and strains and of different sizes and scale patterns from a wide variety of interesting fisheries. I value tremendously the battle of a 20-pounder when it finally lies there glistening in the net after a long stalking session. But I am also just as happy banging into 3 lb wildies or pound-plus crucians one after another on light float tackle. It is all relative.

I hope therefore the reader can share my approach

within the pages of this book, which is far from and in no way pretends to be a complete work on the subject, and quite simply 'catch carp with me'. Perhaps we'll both learn a little along the way.

CHAPTER ONE

THE SPECIES

WILD CARP
(Cyprinus carpio)

Pound for pound there are few fish living in stillwaters to match the speed and the power of the true wild carp. They originated from Eastern Europe and Asia, where the Chinese were the first to cultivate them for food several hundred years before Christ. It was the European monks, however, who brought the species to Britain to rear them in stew ponds for their table. And it is that same race of carp which we today lovingly call 'wildies' or wild carp.

Who knows, one day 'wildie waters' may become a very rare commodity and expensive to fish, because over the years the true wildie has slowly been losing its identity, as more and more fisheries are stocked with the deeper-bodied, heavier and faster-growing strains of king carp.

Although there are slight genetic differences between 'wild' and common, scaled 'king' carp there are no apparent visual differences other than shape. A particularly thin king common, for instance, might just be mistaken for a true wildie (in waters where both exist) while an over-fed wildie can look remarkably like an under-nourished king common. If you are confused you have every right to be, because unless a particular fishery is known to contain only an ancient stock of wild carp to which no other strains have been added, the exact definition of the inhabitants becomes arguable.

However, as there are no separate UK record lists for wild carp – simply 'carp' – regardless of scaleage and ancestry, it really matters not. In any event ultimate weight is nothing like that of the king varieties inhabiting the warmest parts of Europe. Wildies in Britain which weigh in excess of 10 lb are as rare as the proverbial clockwork orange, because the species tends to over-

This long, lean, fully-scaled carp epitomizes the barbel-like shape of the true 'wildie' or wild carp. The true 'wildie' has slowly been losing its identity as more fisheries are stocked with deeper-bodied, faster-growing strains of king carp variants.

populate the shallow, coloured waters where it fares best; farm ponds and irrigation reservoirs being prime examples.

Generally this sleek, barbel-shaped carp averages between 2 and 5 lb as an adult in prolific waters, though naturally fisheries with a lower stock density will produce fish of a higher average size provided the food source is sufficient.

The very reason why wild carp were chosen as an important food source in the first place was that even in overcrowded shallow waters they made the very best of the available food supply and produced per acre far more pounds of edible flesh than any other species.

Presumably for this very reason the same carp was introduced to North America in the 1800s and spread the width and breadth of the continent by the Great Western Railway. Unfortunately, unlike in Europe, carp has never caught on in the USA or Canada as a human food source. Nor has it in the UK, although those of Jewish, Polish, German and Hungarian descent do provide a small market for imported and home-grown table carp.

So 'anti carp' are anglers in the USA and Canada that the fish only rates as enjoyment for lunatics pursuing it with bow and arrow. An abundance of exciting sport-fish species North America may well have, but it is a great pity her fishermen have yet to value the gift of the carp.

When fishing the Red River in Winnipeg, Canada,

during the summers of 1989 and 1990 for the hard-battling channel catfish, I was flabbergasted to hear from my guide, Stu Makay, who runs a tackle business out of Lockport Bridge Dam, that as yet no one has bothered to exploit the fighting potential of the carp as a sport fish in the Red River system. Yet, with its maze of shallow marshlands off the main channel covering hundreds of thousands of acres of water, averaging over 70°F during the summer months, carp are present in unbelievable quantities over 10 lb, and up to 40 lb or more. And they never see a baited hook. Walleye to over 10 lb, white bass to 3 lb, catfish to 30 lb, and various smaller species which make up the fishing potential of the Red River are all held in the highest esteem. But carp – sadly they are considered nothing but vermin.

Small, attractively matured, man-made fisheries originating from gravel excavations are an exciting part of the future of carp fishing within the British Isles.

In Australia, where the introduction of carp to clear, weedy rivers has completely altered the balance and affected the spawning of indigenous species, there is a hefty fine for anyone returning a carp. A similar situation exists in New Zealand, where carp are now breeding prolifically in the ideal conditions of warm, shallow and weedy, slow-moving river systems.

THE KING CARPS
(Cyprinus carpio)

From the original wild carp, different strains have been produced by selective breeding throughout Europe during the past three centuries. In order for the European housewife to be presented with a fast-growing, deep-shouldered table carp, which in some cases (the leather carp) alleviates even the need for descaling, fish culturists have evolved the king carp. This durable carp, due to its fast-growing qualities, massive ultimate weight and attractive scale patterns, forms the basis of British carp fishing as we know it today. For this we owe Germany, Poland, Yugoslavia and Hungary much gratitude. In recent years the Belgians, Israelies, Italians and French have also got in on the act, adding still more variants within the king carp range.

Ultimate weight for a king carp is still uncertain. Monsters of 80 lb plus have been recorded so there is every reason to expect that in the right growing conditions a king carp in excess of 100 lb will one day be taken on rod and line from European waters. In Britain our summers do not get hot enough and are too short for such monsters to be produced, and it is doubtful whether the present ceiling weight of 50 lb will ever be substantially increased. But then with global warming imminent, who really knows for sure.

One of the nicest by-products to come from the selective breeding of king carp strains is the amount of varying scale patterns that occur between the fully-scaled king common carp and the completely scaleless leather carp. We anglers love to catch beautiful fish and the king carp varieties provide both interest and beauty. Carp specialists would perhaps argue about exactly how many varying scaleages can be separately categorized, but there are several distinct patterns. There is of course no way of describing them all, but the following are easily recognizable.

THE KING COMMON CARP is the fully-scaled modern equivalent of the original wild carp, selectively bred to be thicker across the body, deeper and much faster growing with a far greater weight potential.

THE FULLY-SCALED MIRROR, being completely covered in scales of different sizes, is by far the prettiest and possibly the most desirable to catch of all the variants.

THE SCATTER-SCALE MIRROR generally has a continuous line of scales on both sides of the dorsal fin from head to tail, with single or odd groups appearing almost anywhere, particularly close to the tail root or head, or both. By far the most common form of mirror carp.

THE LINEAR MIRROR is known for its straight row of uniform scales along the lateral line, plus odd groups near the tail and on both sides of the dorsal fin.

THE STARBURST MIRROR is really a scatter-scale mirror with a preponderance of tiny, bright scales shot all over the lower half of its body. Italian goldfish and shubunkins have very similar scaleage, reminiscent of a burst of stars – hence this particular carp's nickname.

THE PLATED MIRROR again is really a scatter-scale fish with anything from one to several enormous plate-like scales set in an irregular-shaped group on one or both sides of its body. Not a fish that wears well in a busy fishery, because during the fight the line can catch behind these big scales and force them out.

THE LEATHER CARP is completely free of scales over the body with perhaps the odd line of small scales either side of the dorsal fin.

In addition to scaleage the king carp varies considerably in body shape, but usually has a distinct and characteristic hump between its head and dorsal fin. Those without a hump probably have some wild carp in their ancestry. Certain strains may be long and incredibly thick across the body without having much of an obvious belly, whilst others come short and deep with enormous pot bellies. In truth, there is so much cross-breeding now taking place in the wild as carp propagate all over the country that it would take an experienced carp culturist to be dogmatic about which is truly which. But then the fun of carp fishing lies in fishing waters where you never know what will be coming along next, in size, in shape, in scaleage and even in colour.

Steve Williams from Norwich has every right to look pleased with his capture. This beautifully marked, fully-scaled mirror was caught from a large, heavily reeded Norfolk gravel pit.

COLORATION

Genetic differences apart, colour variation is to some extent governed by the colour of water in which carp live. In sandy or green-pea coloured fisheries, for instance, body coloration often fades to an overall pale, pasty cast in either beige, grey or dull brass with a distinct warm tinge to the tail, pelvic and anal fins. This applies to both wild and king carp, whereas carp inhabiting lush, weedy, clear-watered fisheries can vary along the back from bronze to slate blue, with scales of burnished pewter, gold or silver. The fins will still contain a certain warmth together with hues of grey, purple and beige.

COLOURED VARIANTS
(Metallic Carp)

Actually catching on hook and line a valuable, highly-coloured koi carp would have been unthinkable prior to the mid-1980s. But now, stillwater horizons have broadened due to the general deterioration of river systems caused by abstraction, farming chemicals and increased amounts of sewage effluent. Anglers are ready to accept that king carp/koi crosses or even true koi carp (koi simply

means coloured) can provide exciting sport with beautiful, hard-fighting fish in selected waters. After all, the coloured carps are genetically no different from the original wild carp and share the same latin species name of *cyprinus carpio*.

The Japanese first developed strains of coloured carp, today known as koi. And although there are references in Japanese literature to coloured ornamentals dating back as early as AD 714, the origin of coloured carp is generally accepted to go back to the Hei-an period 794–1184.

Because stillwater fisheries have extended the range of species that they stock over recent years, more and more anglers are now ready to accept that beautiful, hard-fighting fish like this beige-coloured king carp/koi cross can provide exciting sport.

Whatever the scale-age and pigmentation, genetically there is no difference between this beautiful orange hi-goi and all other carp. They all share the Latin name of Cyprinus carpio *and interbreed freely, throwing up all sorts of exciting variations.*

By the Middle Ages, during the Momyama Era from 1582 to 1598, koi culture became popular throughout Japan. Anglers who now have the opportunity of hooking into a koi/king carp cross, the most common of which are called Ghost Koi at fish and garden centres, really have the Japanese to thank.

This stunning breed of 'metallic' carp, so called because most colours suitable for stocking fisheries come in muted shades of metallic pewter, silver, pale gold and burnished beige, are indeed an exciting and extremely durable addition to specialist carp waters.

I stocked metallic carp into my own lakes during the early 1980s and have been more than pleased with the results. Not only do they add another challenge in the range of colour, but seem to know they are 'coloured' and thus more visible. Rarely do the metallics slurp around with their head and shoulders above the surface as uncoloured king carp often do, consuming vast quantities of floaters. Their whole approach – and I can only believe after 10 years of monitoring their antics day in and day out from March to November, that this is typical of metallics – is much more wary. Thus they offer a tremendous challenge, and an alternative to those anglers who fall into the trap of focussing only on the very largest carp, thus denying themselves a glimpse of a breathtakingly coloured 'metallic' in the mesh of their landing-net.

GRASS CARP
(Ctenopharyngoden idella)

This Asian import, which originates from China, adds another exciting chapter to modern stillwater carp fishing, though in appearance the grass carp resembles the chub very closely indeed. Unless its eyes and mouth can be clearly seen, only the fact that it loves to hover just beneath the surface with its head tilted upwards visually distinguishes this sleek battler from chub. Beneath the surface, its tail may also appear to be both darker and slightly larger than that of the chub, but in scaleage they look exactly the same.

The big give-away occurs when it turns head on and

opens its noticeably smaller mouth. The eyes look distinctly odd too. They are in fact set much lower down the head, on a line only just above the jaw hinge.

Grass carp are far from the marauding weed-eaters and nautical lawnmowers they were made out to be when first introduced to the UK. Here, so it seemed, was the answer to everyone's prayers at last, the panacea for anyone who owned a pond or lake dogged with soft weeds. Stock it with a few grass carp and the weeds would be nicely kept in trim – ravaged even.

At least, this was the message from local river authorities and what a load of rubbish it turned out to be. British summers are never long enough, and the water temperature rarely stays high enough for long enough, for the grass carp to become an effective weed-disposal unit. Certainly they consume weed but then so do most cyprinids. The truth is that grass carp are timid when stocked in small numbers into a mature fishery that already contains a prolific stock of king carp, and they always get to the bait last. As they love to feed from the surface, floater-fishing with baits like bread crust or flake on freeline tackle offers the best chance of being selective. They feed from the bottom too, and will accept most common carp baits such as peanuts, boilies, sweetcorn, luncheon meat and so on.

Even when stocked into fisheries that are already densely populated, they will pack on weight and grow to at least double figures within six or seven years. In rich, under-populated stillwaters and rivers, their growth could almost equal that of other carp, and an estimate of 20 lb-plus is not unrealistic.

In Germany, where the grass carp was introduced years ahead of the UK, 40 lb grass carp are not uncommon. As they tend to scrap very well indeed, making long runs close to the surface, who would not fancy the chances of contacting one. Grass carp are the perfect controllable carp for stocking the fisheries of today, because they cannot reproduce in our climate and over-populate a water. As yet, they have not been stocked on a widespread basis, but once fishery owners learn to appreciate their real worth anglers will enjoy them.

It may well be the case in many parts of the country that fishery owners are not even aware that this fine fish exists and that it can be purchased for stocking.

Chub-like in appearance, the enigmatic grass carp freely accept both bottom and surface baits. The downfall of this incredibly long 11-pounder was a small dog-biscuit floater presented on a weighted controller and greased line.

CRUCIAN CARP
(Carassius carassius)

The crucian carp was introduced to the UK sometime during the eighteenth century and has established itself, particularly amongst young anglers, as a popular summer pond fish. It is by far the smallest member of the 'angling carps', rarely exceeding 5 lb. Even this, however, is exceptional. Crucian carp of over 2 lb are considered large specimens because, due to over-breeding, the species becomes stunted and in many waters rarely grows above 12 oz and 10 in in length. This cheeky little carp is noticeably short and deep with distinctly 'rounded' fins. The dorsal is also rounded and convex, in complete contrast to the dorsal fin of other carps which is concave.

The crucian has a small, neat mouth and barbules are absent – one sure way of differentiating between it and either wild or king carp. Coloration tends to vary from one water to another, just like other carp. But they are

Gentle, golden, friendly and decidedly rounded in both body and fins, the crucian might well be the smallest carp around, but it fights doggedly and provides great fun on light tackle.

coloured very evenly in an overall hue of bronze, dull gold or buttery bronze. The fins are also very evenly coloured.

The curious thing about crucians is that they like to shoal in definite age or year groups. So if you catch one weighing, say, 1¼ lb followed by a dozen more, there is an excellent chance that each will be more or less of the same stamp.

This 'peas in the pod' phenomenon can prove a valuable guideline for those seeking out a net full of specimens, though naturally as the fish grow larger the size of the shoal slowly reduces.

CHAPTER TWO

ABOUT CARP

FEEDING

Carp have been likened to aquatic pigs, which is not so very far from the truth. They are by far the most aggressive feeders in freshwater. During a five-month period throughout the winter I reared on in a large, heated aquarium 11 Wels catfish and one mirror carp. Each was around 3 to 4 in long when put in, along with rocks, plants, and sections of drainpipe as refuge for the catfish. I was concerned that the cats would dominate the food introduced, which initially consisted of high protein salmon-fry crumbs, followed by a completely live-fish diet, small gudgeon in fact, netted from the lake into which the cats and carp eventually went.

Invariably it was the lone carp and not the cats which got to the food first – both granulated and live. I was flabbergasted when the first batch of inch-long gudgeon fry were introduced. The mirror carp zoomed up and swallowed 3 live gudgeon before the cats even saw them, and this was more or less what happened every few days at feeding time until I released them into their new home in the spring. By then the cats varied between 11 and 14 in in length and the carp was around 10 in though it was fatter and weighed slightly more than the longest cat. In the wild, wherever both carp and catfish exist together, it is always carp which dominate the available food source and reach your bait first. The balance swings slightly more towards catfish only during darkness, when they naturally become more active, and during high water temperatures – say 70°F and above. But overall and compared to all other freshwater species in Europe, possibly the whole world over, the carp really is the pig of the aquatic scene.

Having said all this, the non-angler may well ask the question, 'Why at times do they become so difficult to catch?' The answer is, that they learn. While carp are not the most intelligent of fish as has been suggested by many specialist fishermen, they quickly learn through association (as all fish do) exactly what to be suspicious about. Baits they have recently been caught on and thus fooled by, over-thick line, insensitive terminal rigs, shadows on the water, unnatural sounds picked up through bank vibrations and so on; these and many other factors, once the carp learns to associate each with danger, are enough to deter it from feeding naturally in its piggy, aggressive way.

I recall an occasion which illustrates this perfectly. During the close season, Neil Pope and Kevin Wilmot from *Angling Times* had arrived at the house to tape part of a series of articles. It was early evening and before we got stuck in around the kitchen table they asked if we could go and feed the carp, something I like to do during the close season to make sure the stock is in good shape for 16th June; and also, I admit, because I simply love to watch fish feeding from the surface. These are carp which for nine months of the year are regularly caught by my 20 syndicate members, but once the close season starts, it doesn't take them long to react to an entirely different set of rules. However, as I walked on ahead to the lake a group of mallards flew from the front lawn to a certain spot on the surface in front of a high, gorse-covered bank, where I stopped. The same spot where, every morning and evening, I throw in a few pints of trout pellets or a bag of old bread scraps.

The carp in the immediate vicinity fully associated the ducks' sudden flight to this particular spot with instant food and quickly gathered around directly beneath them, standing on their tails, mouths open and ready to go. Even before I handed out any pellets or bread scraps, bow waves of additional carp heading through the surface in our direction could be seen on both sides down the lake for as far away as 80 yd. Noise and vibrations travel quickly under water and carp have ears. These distant fish could not possibly have seen or heard *our* arrival 15 ft above, standing well back on the high banking. They were simply reacting to a chain of events, prompted by the arrival of the ducks on the surface at a certain spot and the subsequent movements of other carp to food.

Neil and Kevin stood there absolutely dumbfounded,

There is no doubt about the purpose of the carp's mouth. Complete with thick-rimmed lips and long probing barbules for burrowing deep into the silt to 'feel' for bloodworms and other goodies, it is built to rip the bottom up and turn over vast quantities of organic waste.

obviously assuming I had mystical powers – until I let them in on the situation. After all, no-one expects carp that are caught regularly to appear so quickly. Nevertheless, it's back to square one again on 16th June because suddenly food is being thrown in all over the lake (after being unoccupied for at least three months), and most swims also suddenly have rods hanging threateningly out over the marginal cover. It then takes but a day or two for the fish to revert back to the status quo and to become suspicious again of free food.

This is why you need to be especially stealthy and well camouflaged when tackling previously unfished waters (so-called 'private' lakes where everyone thinks carp crawl up the rods), because if those fish rarely see humans or hear their disturbance along the banks they will be doubly alarmed.

Whilst the carp is capable of obtaining nourishment from almost any food form we offer it, even large baits, its natural diet mostly consists of minute life forms. With its

two pairs of barbules – one long pair at the corner of the mouth, which is protusible, and the other, short ones on the upper lip – the carp is a past master at seeking out midge larvae (blood worms) and annelid worms from the deepest silt concentrations. Deep craters 3 to 6 ft across can sometimes be observed through the clear water of shallow, silty lakes, where concentrations of midge larvae are richest. The carp have simply excavated them whilst feeding, their head and shoulders almost buried while the barbules, which have sensitive taste pads at the tips, 'feel' for the worms. Occasionally a carp may come up to the surface to take floaters, covered in fine mud all over its head; proof that shortly before, it was merrily rooting about in the silt with its head buried, feeding on midge larvae and sending those tell-tale feeding bubbles up to the surface.

When sifting through bottom silt in the early morning, carp send streams of bubbles up to the surface. Follow the route of individual fish feeding at close range, and you can catch them on a simple float rig by casting a little to one side of the rising bubbles.

These bubbles are caused by two things: gases which escape from the detritus (the rotting layer of vegetation on the bottom); and those created by the carp itself as it crushes up its food with its pharyngeal teeth (throat teeth), emitting the bubbles through its gills. Observing the bubbles of feeding carp is one of the most accurate ways of locating them and arranging subsequent bait presentation (more about this in 'Locating Carp').

The carp also uses its flat, immensely powerful pharyngeal teeth for crushing the shells of molluscs upon which it feeds – the tiny pea mussel, snails and even the considerably larger swan mussel. Shells of 2 to 3 in long are light work for the carp's throat teeth, releasing the succulent meat inside. Small dead and live fish up to 6 in long are also easily minced, as anglers offering them after dark with the intention of luring catfish or eels have discovered.

In prolifically stocked waters, especially where competition for the natural aquatic food is high, carp consume far more fish than most anglers could imagine. During the spawning season it is natural for them to munch away on both the spawn and newly-hatched fry. And this does not stop them from enjoying larger 'small fish' either dead or alive at any time of the year. In North America during the summer months, when water temperatures are considerably higher than in the UK, carp are caught regularly on spinners, spoons and jigs, suggesting perhaps that they become more aggressive predators the warmer the water becomes.

Other favourite natural foods are all aquatic insects and beetles, shrimps, assellus and a certain amount of algae from silt and mud on the bottom. They will also gorge on the largest of the zoo planktons, the daphnia, when they are present in thick clouds. As a food converter the carp surpasses even the gluttony of the trout.

Crucians

By comparison with both wild and king carp, the crucian is very timid and deliberate in its feeding. Its diet is not dissimilar to the larger carp at the smaller end of the food chain, and it manages to eke out a living and even to compete with them in densely populated fisheries. I know of many so called 'fast' carp waters which are densely populated with either wildies, king carp or both, but where only crucian carp appear to maintain their existence in quite bagable numbers, whereas either tench or bream as a second species would simply be eaten out of house and home by the larger carp. Perhaps the crucians are simply better at exploiting the smaller food chains than all the other species. They can bite oh-so-gently however, even on light float tackle.

Owing to the crucian carp's slightly upturned mouth structure, they need to stand on their heads (just like the tench) when sucking up food from the bottom. And on chewing it with their pharyngeal teeth they emit distinctive 'crucian bubbles', which rise to the surface in small groups. Ardent crucian fishermen could not mistake these bubbles for any other fish. The bubbles probably fall halfway between those of tench and the larger carps in size, and are never 'frothy'.

REPRODUCTION

In the British Isles carp have the capacity to spawn at any time between early May and the end of July, depending on water temperature. In sheltered, shallow lakes not affected by cold winds, for instance, where the water warms quickly, carp are most likely to spawn early. Whereas in large open and very deep-watered gravel pits which take a long time to warm up, spawning may not occur until even the end of July. This of course makes a nonsense of the dates for the statutory close season, because it is mostly water temperature which prompts fish to shed their eggs.

It is perhaps a blessing in disguise that in the UK a large percentage of the spawn does not reach adulthood, which is far from the case in countries like Australia, North America and Spain for instance, or our fisheries would simply be overrun with carp to the detriment of other species.

When spawning occurs, the spectator can have little doubt it is happening. It is a very noisy event, particularly when every fish in the lake seems bent on propagation at the same time. Propagation usually starts in the early hours and continues until the sun gets high; it may resume again during the evening. The activity continues every morning for several days, unless the weather changes drastically with a sharp fall in temperature. Then spawning ceases, sometimes for many weeks, until carp feel the urge again, stimulated by a steady rise in water temperature.

During poor summers and continually long cold spells

The carp's pharyngeal teeth are situated between its gill plates at the back of the throat, and are used for grinding food to a pulp. This pair was taken from a dead fish slightly larger than the mirror carp shown here.

some females never get to shed their eggs, resulting in hideous pot-bellied fish which can eventually die from their spawn-bound condition unless they manage to re-absorb the eggs into their system. Each ripe female is usually accompanied by anywhere from two to several males, all eager to spray milt over the eggs as she sheds them amongst the fibrous sub-surface roots of marginal trees, through rushes, sedges, reeds, lilies, soft weeds and so on. This is accompanied by much audible shuddering and splashing as the entwining carp crash their way through marginal vegetation where the water is warmest. Such is the force of the males' attention that the female is often lifted bodily out of the water, while the odd over-zealous male can even find itself high and dry on the bank.

The sticky eggs are each about the size of a no. 8 split shot, and are a translucent pale colour unless they failed to receive milt from the male, in which case they remain unfertilized and quickly turn white. Eggs that are not quickly consumed by shoals of small roach, perch or rudd, which follow the spawning carp in anticipation, or by the carp themselves, hatch some six to ten days later. Again this depends on the amount of sunlight and subsequent water

temperature. The newly-hatched fry have yolk sacks to feed on for two to four days before coming to the surface and filling their swim bladders with air. They then become free swimming and commence feeding on microscopic life.

If a lake contains a varied stock of mixed carp, inter-breeding occurs when they all get together at spawning time. Wildies spawn with kings, crucians with wildies, wildies with metallic king mirrors or leather or commons, and so on.

The wildie/crucian carp cross matures into an interesting fish which appears slightly too deep to be the true wildie everyone assumes it is, the give-away being its noticeably smaller barbules and an overall paler coloration.

The most attractive crosses of all come from the metallic carps with koi ancestry locked up in their genes. Most of the brightest ones never get beyond the fry stage. Being far more visible than the rest, they soon fall prey to the stealthy heron and predatory fish. But those that are only slightly tinted over the body and on the underside of the pectoral and pelvic fins in shades of muted silver and beige turn into breathtaking carp, particularly those with mirror scaleage.

Carp in the British Isles are so interbred that with most it is virtually impossible to state the exact parentage. This golden metallic mirror cross, however, obviously has koi ancestry.

DISTRIBUTION

Although there are still 'wildie only' waters in Wales, southern England and the Midlands, few exist in Scotland and Ireland. On the other hand, king carp and their variants are now being stocked into just about every new lake or gravel pit fishery through the North, the Midlands and southern England. Not that carp really need any help at this stage. They have steadily spread (and not always by the design of water authorities) into numerous river systems all over the country. The Trent, Thames and the Great Ouse are prime examples where carp are now so prolific in certain stretches that anglers can actually pick a swim known for producing numbers of them, something that was virtually unheard of in this country's rivers only 20 years ago.

The crucian does not spread so readily, and fares poorly in running water. It is, however, becoming increasingly popular amongst match and club fishermen because it is extremely durable, and it exists in prolific numbers even in diminutive stillwater fisheries.

CHAPTER THREE

LOCATING CARP

M AKE no mistake about it, carp location is what catching them is really all about. After all, if there are none where you place the bait, you can't catch them. So be willing, and this applies in particular to fisheries low in carp stocks and large areas of water, to spend more hours in locating the fish than you do actually fishing.

Tools of the trade, as important as the rod and reel, are polaroid glasses, binoculars, drab clothing and lightweight boots, whether waterproof or not, so that from the very start your approach is not at fault. The importance of being quiet, stealthy and unseen against the skyline cannot be stressed enough if you wish to find and subsequently study your quarry before offering it a bait. When you can creep up (crawl if necessary) to within a few feet of carp, or watch them swim close by without their having the slightest inkling of your presence, you should then be qualified to catch them from any type of water. No other fish except the chub demands such cautionary measures but it is an apprenticeship in watercraft that when learnt will last a lifetime.

SMALL STILLWATERS

Where carp cannot be bodily observed because the water is too coloured or temperatures too cold for them to be basking on the surface, there are many pointers to look for. Fortunately carp love features, gravel bars, sunken trees, lily pads, reedlines, etc., and are never far away. In diminutive waters, ponds, pits, meres, lakes – those for argument's sake of less than 3 acres (a football pitch is about 1 acre) – carp are not difficult to locate, and are fun

Careful observation is paramount if you wish to catch carp with regularity from a wide range of stillwaters. Owning a pair of binoculars and climbing the occasional tree is not cheating, but be careful.

to study. Nearly always they can be visually tracked down during the summer months. The most obvious indication of fish is the characteristic way in which carp 'bubble' (see 'Feeding'). Their 'feeding bubbles', which could occur at any time of the day (especially during overcast, humid, thundery oppressive summer weather), are most likely to appear coinciding with dawn. They could well then continue until the sun's rays fall directly on the water. This post-dawn feeding period is by far the heaviest. More importantly, it pin-points areas which carp visit often, usually on a day-to-day basis, and most important of all where they feed 'naturally'.

Simply taking time for a stealthy stroll with a pair of binoculars at dawn can provide so much information, far more in fact than an entire week of midday sessions. What stands out when observing 'bubbles' is that many natural feeding areas are situated ridiculously close in. That's because shallow water warms up quickly and invariably contains per square foot a much richer larder of natural food, a fact of which carp quickly become aware. This is the reason margin fishing under quiet conditions can prove

so effective. Why so many carp fishermen cast right over to the other bank when they could just as easily (probably more effectively too) walk round and catch the same fish beneath the rod tip on considerably lighter, more enjoyable tackle, is completely beyond my comprehension. Certainly, once they have been scared away from their preferred haunts a long cast is necessary to offer them a bait. The object, however, is not to scare them away in the first place.

Find lilies and you will find carp. In this green jungle, amongst a mixture of dwarf pond lily and large pads of the common yellow water lily, a fat mirror and a mallard cross see who can reach the floaters first.

Lilies

Lily-beds, the thicker the better, are the most popular of the carp's daytime haunts, especially in waters with little protection to offer in the way of overhanging trees and marginal growth. The shade provided by pads overhead and a maze of roots below, to which a rich supply of snails and their eggs adhere, makes these sub-surface vegetable gardens very attractive.

Fortunately, the vast majority of anglers feel inhibited about trying to extract such a large fish as carp from dense vegetation, so thick beds of lilies remain largely unexplored. The ideal outfit consists of a stretchy line and all–through-action rod for subduing the heavy lunges of a hooked fish.

Whether carp are present or not is sometimes plainly obvious, their wide backs pushing pads, flowers and stalks aside as they forage beneath. There will be occasions, however, when it seems there isn't a carp anywhere near the lilies. However, take a long slow look. Don't trust the naked eye; rely on the magnification provided by bin-oculars, even for scanning beds of lilies situated close in. Look for the single flower stalk that sways gently when there is no wind; for large bubbles rising to the surface in groups of just two or three; for the fry shoal which suddenly scatters across the surface, not followed by a predatory perch or pike; for patches of discoloured water (these are evident through polaroids in even the most coloured waters) beneath the pads, alongside or even several yards away.

Climb a suitable tree close by for the best possible view of the situation. If you stay up in the branches long enough and are able to observe carp entering a large bed of lilies, it will eventually become obvious that they go in only at certain spots. These are the wide, naturally formed entrances to the tunnels through the maze of stems and rhyzomes which the carp navigate – worth remembering when you are back down on the ground again, wondering where to plop in a bait.

Owing to its extra, sub–surface leaves, the common yellow water lily (*Nuphar lutea*) is much preferred by carp to the white and coloured cultivated varieties wherever they have a choice. But once hooked, fish are more difficult to extract from the tough stems and enormous entanglement of tubers, which often 'suspend' well above the bottom.

Miniature surface plants such as the dwarf pond lily (easily identified by its buttercup–yellow flowers and perfectly round pads rarely exceeding 3 in across) and the oval–shaped, broad–leaved pond weed (with its erect pink seed–heads protruding above the surface) both also attract carp like bees to a honey pot. Find extensive beds of either smothering the surface of any small (or large) stillwater and expect carp to be foraging beneath at some time during the day, if not all day long.

Sunken/overhanging trees

The presence of carp should always be expected beneath overhanging branches and those which actually trail the surface, because they love a roof over their heads during the hottest, brightest part of a summer's day. Whole trees or large foliage-covered limbs actually sunk below the surface provide fabulous hot spots all year through.

Sunken willows and alders in particular sprout, enormous, fibrous root structures which are teeming with aquatic insect larvae. They provide carp with both food and a retreat where the light from above is always diffused. It is no coincidence that the biggest carp in small waters choose to live in the snaggiest habitats.

Reed lines

Tall marginal plants best loved by carp are the common reed, reed mace (wrongly called bullrush due to its cigar-like seed heads), and the lesser reed mace, a slimmer version. Each will attract carp for the natural food which clings to the upright stems, provided there is a depth of 18 in of water or more. Thick beds of reed which from the front line reach back several yards into marsh bog with pockets of open water in between are great locations, where carp can be expected to browse at any time of the day. And the tall willowy stems even conveniently 'knock' together betraying the presence of any carp moving or feeding between them. Wild carp especially, due to their round profile, are tailor-made for working alongside and through beds of reed.

Gravel bars and shallow plateaux

Owing to the uneven way in which gravel and sand deposits were originally laid down during the last Ice Age, when these minerals are being excavated poor seams are left. Once the pit is allowed to flood from the water table, these seams eventually appear as islands, shallow bars or plateaux. And to each of these carp automatically become

In a quiet corner of a small lake heavily overgrown with branches a sizeable carp buckles the rod, having sucked up the insides of a whole swan mussel freelined beneath the overhanging foliage. Note how the angler has submerged the rod tip to lower the angle of the line so it stands less chance of snagging, and to apply side strain.

In this swim John practises what he preaches by using the marginal reedline of a shallow, clear-water lake as camouflage. He is offering a bait on the noses of carp that are working close in, feeding on aquatic insects clinging to the upright stems.

attracted. Narrow gaps situated between islands, for instance, could become part of their daily feeding route. Not all, but a proportion of shallow bars will provide either a canopy of floating plants with shelter beneath, or a larder of shrimps and snails amongst the gravel, thus attracting carp. Deeper bars, situated about 4 to 6 ft beneath the surface but 'bars' none the less (where the bottom shelves down to twice the depth or more on either side), are particularly favoured and are ideal locations for pre-baiting. Sometimes these can be seen and pinpointed from the bank through clear water, sometimes not.

Either way, it pays to put in a good amount of reconnaisance work with a plummet (use a boat during the close season if one is allowed at the fishery) when locating carp from a previously unfished or unexplored pit. Discovering the exact whereabouts of all the bars and large areas of plateaux is the absolute key to where carp are most likely to feed naturally.

LARGE STILLWATERS

Though seemingly more daunting because the action of strong winds rippling the surface destroys many of the easily recognizable points which aid location in small fisheries, there is in fact a similarity of approach to tackling the carp of large lakes and gravel pits. And the first step is to think of a large pit as nothing more than a collection of features, just like several small pits joined together. You isolate in your mind (with the help of a drawing if you prefer) all those previously mentioned features to which carp are attracted; the bars, routes between groups of islands, shorelines with dense reed beds, bays harbouring surface plants, overhanging and sunken trees, deep gullies with shallow water on either side and so on. Then spend time with the binoculars during reasonable weather conditions when there is a chance of locating fish visually, not during a raging gale.

A great way of locating carp at any time throughout the summer, especially when it is very warm and they are more liable to be close to the surface of generally deep waters, is to attract them up with floaters. From the

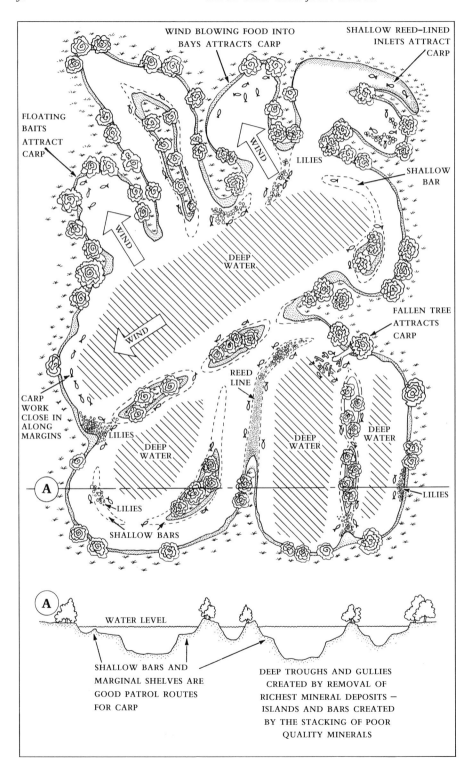

WIND BLOWING FOOD INTO
BAYS ATTRACTS CARP

SHALLOW REED–LINED
INLETS ATTRACT
CARP

FLOATING
BAITS
ATTRACT
CARP

LILIES

SHALLOW
BAR

WIND

DEEP
WATER

WIND

FALLEN TREE
ATTRACTS
CARP

WIND

REED
LINE

CARP
WORK
CLOSE IN
ALONG
MARGINS

LILIES

DEEP
WATER

DEEP
WATER

DEEP
WATER

LILIES

A

LILIES

SHALLOW BARS

A

WATER LEVEL

SHALLOW BARS AND
MARGINAL SHELVES ARE
GOOD PATROL ROUTES
FOR CARP

DEEP TROUGHS AND GULLIES
CREATED BY REMOVAL OF
RICHEST MINERAL DEPOSITS –
ISLANDS AND BARS CREATED
BY THE STACKING OF POOR
QUALITY MINERALS

furthest up-wind position on the bank catapult the surface with small floaters, chum mixers or cat biscuits, and allow the wind to drift this new food source down to the other end of the fishery. Don't be mean during these initial location sessions because they can provide great fun towards the end of the close season when you are itching to see carp. Water birds, like swans, cootes, moorhens and mallards all recognize and come to like floaters unfortunately, so you want enough on the surface to bring the carp up and satisfy the water birds. The presence of birds on the surface enjoying floaters, anyway, is not entirely a bad thing (see 'Feeding'). It gives confidence to the carp below if they are initially hesitant, to a point where eventually they cannot resist getting in on the act. It is that competitive element within all living creatures. Carp may locate and start to feed on the floaters at any time during the drift, especially those which catch up amongst soft weedbeds touching the surface, lilies, or against marginal vegetation. On the other hand, they may not show the slightest interest until the floaters have completed the full length of the fishery and finally come to rest in a scum line hugging the windward shoreline – one very good reason why that old adage of 'fishing into the wind' can prove a winner.

Scumlines

Thick scumlines of pollen, twigs, leaves and other bits formed by the wind blowing from the same direction for several days are great attractors. Natural food including clouds of zooplanktons such as daphnia, plus the remnants of floating fishing baits, are all concentrated in a soup in one area. If this happens to be a shoreline already blessed with features like thick beds of marginal reeds or sedges, lilies or partly submerged trees, it could attract carp in surprising numbers and hold them there until the wind changes direction. On large 'featureless' waters, wind direction alone usually dictates where all small items of natural foods held in suspension near the surface will eventually be deposited. This is why varying areas attract carp only at certain times. These deposits often come to rest on the leeward side of islands and promontories (see

Opposite FIGURE 1
A gravel pit seen from the surface and (bottom) *in cross-section, showing the gullies and patrol routes of the carp.*

Consisting of leaves, pollen, twigs and dead insects, blown into the margins by the wind, scumlines are known for attracting carp. Keeping down amongst the foliage, well camouflaged by a thick clump of young alders, this angler presents floaters to carp patrolling the scumline.

fig. 1) just as silt in flowing water sinks to the bottom downstream and on the inside of bends where the current always slows down. And whilst the feeding bubbles of carp cannot easily be seen rising in these natural larders at great distances, fish often roll or jump completely clear of the surface when feeding actively and give away their position.

Look closely also for any large 'flat' or calm areas several feet square which suddenly appears amongst the waves. These 'calms' are caused by carp moving beneath the surface without actually breaking it. Such is the force created by their body displacement and powerful fins, the surface tension is 'flattened' long enough for it to be picked up through binoculars even at great distances.

Carp which cannot be seen through really heavily coloured water, even when they feed close in along shallow margins, also indicate their presence through water displacement called 'tail patterns'. These spiral up to the surface in minute vortexes when the carp stands on its head to feed, waggling its tail gently from side to side. Sometimes these 'tail patterns' are accompanied by feeding bubbles and even the fish's body breaking surface, but not always. All are visual indications not to be missed.

Depths

Carp are sometimes stocked into and caught from waters of great depth (20 ft or more) that are completely devoid of shallow areas. However, where they are given a choice of varying depths at which to feed (most waters), I would suggest they prefer to spend a much greater part of their time in less than 12–14 ft of water, rather than deeper water. This is because the greatest concentrations of natural food and choice plant habitats are produced in part by sunlight. And in excessively deep water, particularly if it is heavily coloured (old clay pits and the like), sunlight cannot penetrate down far enough to stimulate growth.

WINTER LOCATION

Though the leaves have gone, over-hanging trees beneath which carp basked all summer are the first spots to try once winter sets in and frosts clear the water. At midday during maximum visibility, their dark shapes can often be seen among the sunken branches.

Many prime summer haunts will still hold carp through-out the winter months, particularly dense habitat areas where partly submerged trees and bushes overhang the margins into deepish water. Deep gullies or troughs in what are generally shallow lakes or pits are also certain to be holding fish.

The much deeper, 'dam' end of man-made estate-type lakes is the obvious choice in continually cold conditions. Even lily beds (or what's left of them) maintain their attraction for carp despite the rotting stalks, and pads not being visible. Always keep a mental note (by lining up a particular tree or gate post on the opposite bank during the summer when the pads are up) as to exactly where the main structure of the plants are situated for winter attention. Carp will always be found amongst it.

RIVER CARP

These are really a law unto themselves. Although they are naturally attracted to all features associated with flowing water, like weir pools, lock cuttings, junctions where side streams join the main flow, mill streams, deep holes on acute bends, beneath overhanging trees and so on, they are completely nomadic, travelling long distances in the course of just a few hours.

Most of the carp in my local Norfolk rivers, the Yare, Wensum and Waveney (which were not intentionally stocked, but contain escapees from fish farms and gravel-pit fisheries adjacent to the rivers) are great wanderers. I have caught them on ledgered bread flake whilst winter chubbing, and right out of the blue during the autumn when barbel fishing swims that have been heavily pre-baited with hemp seed. They are also hooked (and occasionally even landed) by matchmen on casters on maggots designed for roach in the tidal stretches.

In short, one might turn up by itself, or as one of a small group, from just about anywhere and at any time. I have occasionally managed to bag one instantly whilst playing the wandering game for chub, using freelined lobworms in the clear weedy conditions of summer. However, river carp are not keen to respond to an 'instant' meal plopped close by, as chub do. Such offerings are treated with far more suspicion.

River carp do, however, respond wonderfully to regular pre-baiting and this is the most successful way of locating them. The ruse is to pick a few likely habitat-type swims where carp are occasionally seen, and then every other day introduce some loose feed. Stewed wheat, peanuts, maize (don't forget to pressure cook it), black eyed beans and so on (see 'Baits') are all cheap enough to purchase in bulk for heavy and regular baitings. Taking into account the fact that water birds and unwanted species like chub will quickly try and mop up much of the bait, it is pointless putting in just the odd handful. We are talking about something like 3 to 6 pt a go, otherwise you are simply wasting your time and money, as you would be if you used baits such as maggots which every other fish gobbles up long before the carp arrive on the scene.

LOCATING CRUCIANS

This is a most pleasant exercise in the confines of small fisheries (and most crucian waters are small), due to the fact that they conveniently bubble away (see 'Feeding') from dawn onwards between June and September. They feed well into sunlight, even all day through on occasions, so long as the loose feed keeps going in.

They are so obliging and love to porpoise on the surface when in a feeding mood, particularly at dawn and dusk. They are also known for those spectacular jumps completely clear of the surface. Why they do this has never been fully understood, but I have always suspected they are simply ridding themselves of parasites from their gills or scales after sifting through bottom mud and silt.

Look for their distinctive bubbles in warm, shallow to medium-depth swims between beds of any floating-leaved plant, lilies especially (though broad-leaved pond weed, amphibious bistort and dwarf pond lily are also much loved by them) and you will have located the choicest of crucian habitats.

Where there are no lilies, explore just a few feet out from the reedline or close alongside partly submerged bushes

(blackthorn, hawthorn, brambles, etc.) which grow out over the water and actually hang their foliage beneath the surface. Look for definite habitats, but above all from that 'pregnant dawn period' look for those groups of feeding bubbles.

Because crucians, unlike the larger carps, rarely roam to follow food lines, most fisheries have 'known' crucian carp swims or hot spots where these obliging fish reside day in, day out regardless of angling pressure. Mind you, such fish learn to be incredibly crafty, and become the most delicately biting fish in freshwater. So the location of new and not so popular areas is a worthwhile exercise.

Crucian carp love the warm, shallow, lily-shaded water of small lakes, pits and meres. Sometimes you need look no further than the village pond.

River carp are naturally attracted to weir pools, and are fun to catch wherever you fish. During filming for his TV series, when Go Fishing visited Spain and the mighty River Ebro, John located numbers of common carp running into double figures just off the main channel in a tiny, rocky overshoot pool. On freelined bread flake trundled around in the turbulence, bites were not slow in coming.

CHAPTER FOUR

TACKLE

DURING the 1980s more specialized tackle was marketed to feed the growing demand for carp fishing than for any other branch of fishing in the UK ever. Carp fishing has indeed become big business. Unfortunately, newcomers to the sport often suffer under the illusion that unless they are equipped with all the latest gadgetry they won't catch carp, which is simply not true.

RODS

Test curves

Rods designed and sold specifically for carp fishing usually have a 'test curve' rating printed along with the manufacturer's logo immediately above the handle. This provides a guide to the rod's power and therefore suggested line strengths to go with it so that both rod and line stretch in harmony like one enormous elastic band. To find out the suggested line strength for a particular rod you simply multiply its test curve rating by 5. For instance – a test curve of 2 lb will result in an ideal line strength of around 10 lb. It is as simple as that. To find the lower limit of lines that can safely be used with a rod, multiply by 4 (8 lb test) and by 6 for the upper limit (12 lb test).

These figures of course offer only a general guideline, because in experienced hands far lighter and heavier lines could be used in special circumstances with the same rod. But there has to be a better yardstick than judging the power of a rod purely by its looks, and as yet no one has improved on the test curve principle. Incidentally the words 'test curve' relate to the strain (in lbs) required to pull the rod's tip into a quarter circle, a method devised originally for rods made of built-cane which had an all-through progressive action.

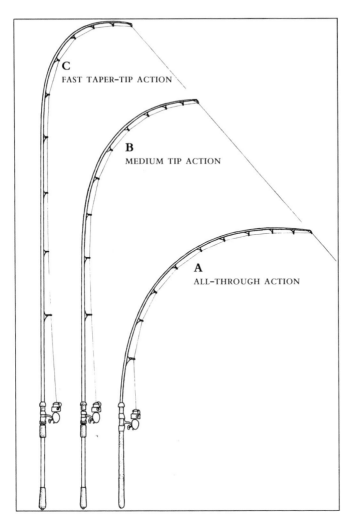

FIGURE 2 *Carp rod actions*

Action

In addition to the rod's power, its action must also be considered. Most rods fall roughly into one of three popular categories. Rods which (similar to built-cane) bend progressively along their length, into a full curve under maximum load are described as *all-through action* (fig. 2A). Those whose action is mostly in the upper half or tip section are called *medium tip action* (fig. 2B). Rods where only the upper tip really bends to any degree are called *fast taper* (fig. 2C). All-through action rods are

For fishing at close range and for subduing large carp in overgrown parts of the fishery, rods with an all-through action are imperative. They absorb the fish's lunges, while the line stretches in complete harmony.

designed for close-in situations and for fishing at reasonably short range, say distances of up to 30/40 yd. Beyond this, for picking up the line and subsequently setting the hook when striking at greater distances, up to say 70/80 yd, a 'medium tip action' is the tool for the job. This is probably the most useful all-round actioned carp rod. To cope with still greater distances, 90 yd plus (far more specialized fishing), a fast taper-action rod is needed. However, because a fast taper rod bends very little other than in the extreme tip, you need to be especially careful not to rip out the hook or snap the line when bringing a heavy fish to the net on the end of a short line.

Nowadays, few carp rods are manufactured from either built-cane or fibre-glass. Carbon fibre, with various strengthening and shock absorbing agents added such as 'Kevlar', has more or less taken over the specialist market, resulting in rods of a very narrow profile which, in addition to being immensely strong, are pleasantly light to use. Rods by Daiwa, Ryobi, North Western Blanks, Tri Cast and Century Composites fall into this category.

Length

While two-piece 13 ft 'specials' are perhaps necessary for ultra-long-range carp fishing, most carp rods are produced in either 11 or 12 ft models. For picking up line at distance and for overall carp fishing into deep waters I would suggest that a 12-footer is absolutely ideal. For all close-range work, casting and playing fish beneath overhanging trees, fishing overgrown jungle-type swims, etc., the standard length of 11 ft is perfect. In fact an 11-footer with a test curve of somewhere between 1¾–2 lb (taking lines 8–10 lb test) is as close to the ideal rod as you could get.

A word at this point is perhaps in order about handle length, or more accurately where the screw reel fitting is positioned, because far too many rods have the reel fitting placed higher up the handle than is necessary. It may look very trendy, but what is the point in having a foot of rod sticking out beyond your elbow when playing a fish. Not only is the rod's effective length reduced by·this amount, it

The ideal rod for striking the delicate bites of crucian carp and enjoying the fight they give, is a 13-ft match rod. Those designed with an 'easy' action for fishing the waggler are highly recommended.

is impossible to lay the rod over for applying sidestrain if the butt is so long it cannot be moved easily across your stomach. A good guide to the ideal distance is the length of a hand grip (at the bottom end) added to the length of your forearm and hand. The reel should then fit immediately below your hand. For the average adult this varies between 21 and 24 in from butt cap to reel stem – no more.

Rods for crucians

To the best of my knowledge there has never been a rod designed or marketed solely for the purpose of catching crucian carp. This is no doubt due to the market for such a rod being very small, coupled with the fact that any 12 or 13 ft match-come-float rod suitable for taking roach or bream is ideally suited to catching crucians.

REELS

The main requirement of any fixed-spool reel used for carp fishing is that it should have a wide spool so that the line comes off in large loose coils, as opposed to tight coils which restrict casting and bait presentation. Also, the spool should hold enough line, say 200 yd of 8/10 or 12 lb test mono. A super-fast retrieve is not required; I repeat – not required. The playing of fish is much smoother with a reel of standard gear ratio. A sensitive clutch, however, is of paramount importance if, like me, you prefer to play fish using the clutch.

In recent years the tactic of tightening the clutch right down and backwinding to play the fish through the gears instead of the clutch has been popularized by many specialist anglers. I would suggest, however, that by learning to use the clutch for the purpose it was designed for – by setting it properly so that the spool rotates and gives line before reaching full load – remains the most efficient way of ensuring that a big fish takes no more line than you actually need to give. And for controlling fish hooked close to, or actually right in among snaggy swims, this is very important.

You simply tighten the drag knob until line can just be pulled firmly yet smoothly from the spool – no more, no less. This of course prompts the question, which type of reel is best: reels with a standard front-adjusting clutch (built into the spool itself), as in the legendary Mitchell 300 and 400 range of reels; or the more recent skirted-spool, rear-drag reels, a format most manufacturers now seem to be producing. Unfortunately it is a question I cannot answer because the choice is a very personal one. I do in fact use both types. Skirted-spool reels do not allow line to slip down and become tangled between spool and the rotor housing; in addition, because the drag knob is situated at the rear or bottom of the reel, clutch adjustment even whilst playing a fish is found easier by the majority of fishermen. On the other hand, front drags are far less complicated; they have fewer parts to wear, and less torque on the system because only the spool turns and not the rotor.

In recent years many innovative creations have been added to fishing reels, including electronic wizardry, such as mini bite alarms which bleep and light up as the spool rotates and line is taken – though these have yet to catch on. Something that has become an important feature to carp anglers, however, in particular those presenting baits on heavy leaded shock or bolt rigs (see 'Bolt rig ledgering', p. 115) is the 'baitrunner' design patented by 'Shimano' which, through a trip lever, allows the spool to be completely disengaged from the drag system. Thus, a carp belting off is allowed to do so with the bale arm in the closed position as the spool rotates freely. There is even a separate 'spool drag' for when the baitrunner facility is in operation. Simply by turning the handle again the spool is returned to its pre-set drag and disengaged the baitrunner lever.

At the end of the day, you get what you pay for. So above all, invest in a good-quality reel, as opposed to one crammed with gimmicks. It should have a strong bale arm that incorporates a roller which actually rotates as the line pulls across it (to obviate excess friction), and it should be smooth in operation. Those which run on two or three sets of ball bearings, as do top-of-the-range models by ABU, Shimano, Ryobi, Mitchell and Daiwa, are highly recommended. For catching crucian carp, where close-range fishing with much lighter lines is the order of the day, choose a miniature fixed-spool with a super-sensitive clutch or a centre pin. Both allow the fight of crucians to be enjoyed to the full.

LINES

Contrary to all the advertising hype accompanying every new line as it arrives on the market, very little has changed with monofilament line during the last few decades. This is possibly because it is, quite simply, a commodity which can be developed no further. It is now as abrasion-resistant, as fine and as supple, with a suitable degree of stretch, as it is ever going to be. The plain truth is that if you pre-stretch monofilament of a certain test and dia-

When endeavouring to catch heavy-weight carp at close range, such as this 27 lb leather, do not put your trust in a low-stretch line. Thinner, pre-stretched lines have greatly reduced elasticity and will part when you most need a shock absorber.

meter, it will become that much thinner and therefore easier to fool the carp with. But at what price – and this is what everyone seems to forget – because it will then have greatly reduced elasticity, and it is the elastic-band action, or 'stretch', of regular monofilament that permits the landing of big fish on light lines.

Remove the 'buffer', as has happened with so-called revolutionary, much thinner lines (which have been reduced to minimal stretch) and the line parts just when you don't want it to: with the fish thumping away beneath the rod tip on a short line, about to be netted. It has been my experience as a tackle dealer, even after warning carp anglers of the consequences, that more have parted company with big fish hooked on low-diameter, pre-stretched lines than for any other reason.

Having said all this, low-diameter pre-stretched monofilament does make excellent hook lengths. A thinner line tied to the hook is bound to encourage more bites, especially when presenting floaters or fishing in clear water. Only when fishing at extreme range, however, (100 yd plus) would I ever consider filling the reel with a pre-stretched line; and then only because regular mono, due to its inherent stretch, inhibits hook penetration on the strike.

I have for very many years relied upon Sylcast (in sorrel) and Maxima Chameleon for all my carp fishing. Both are consistently smooth, have just the right amount of stretch and are extremely supple. When I am winding new line straight on to the reel, I increase its suppleness by removing any coil caused by being stored on spools. This 'relaxing' process makes fishing with brand new line a pleasure instead of a nightmare because the 'spring' has been taken out. After filling up the spool and fixing the reel to the rod, thread the line through the rings and tie a large loop on the end. Slip it over a gate post or something similar and walk 30 yd away. Then wind gently down and slowly bend the rod into a full curve, holding it there for several seconds. Now point the rod at the fence post and wind until the line is tight to the reel with the rod straight. Walk slowly backwards a few paces 'feeling' just how much stretch there is in new monofilament. When it is really tight, obviously long before full elasticity is reached, hold it there for ten seconds. Afterwards, it can be wound back onto the spool nicely limp and ready for work. This may sound a bit of a rigmarole but I can assure you it is well worth the effort.

HOOK LENGTHS

In addition to using both regular and pre-stretched monofilament for the hook length, the suppleness of braided dacron makes it a fine alternative. In fact, all kinds of braided hook lengths are available to carp fishermen, from the standard black, low-stretch but incredibly supple braided dacron (also available camouflaged and flecked) to the multi-strands like Gamastrand floss and Kryston, both of which separate on the bottom into numerous gossamer single strands. The latter gives the carp greater confidence in accepting the bait with the advantage that the multi-strands return to one unit and full strength for striking and playing the fish.

HOOKS

Because it is the final link connecting you to what could be the carp of a lifetime, think seriously about the type and strength of hook when buying them. Never buy in-expensive hooks, or simply ask the tackle dealer for a packet of size 8 eyed hooks. In complete innocence he could be thinking of his customer's pocket and hand over cheapies which bend or spring open under minimal pressure. What you need is a hook that can be totally relied upon, forged with either a bronze or black finish, and chemically sharpened or etched to a needle point (keep a small stone handy for ensuring they stay sharp). My favourite hooks for heavy fishing are the Drennan super specialist and the Mustad 34021 O'Shaunessy patterns. In these I have complete confidence, whether cranking in a whopper from a jungle swim or taking it easy with medium-sized carp hooked in a completely snag-free environment.

For really light carping when stepping down to, say, 6 lb test for presenting floating baits to shy fish in clear

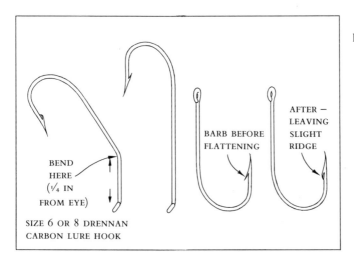

FIGURE 3 *Hooks*

water, or going even lighter with a reel line of 2½ lb test tied direct to the hook for catching crucians, then the Drennan carbon specimen range fits the bill perfectly. In sizes 12 to 8 these particular hooks are fine enough in the wire not to inhibit carp from sucking up the bait, yet strong enough to stay in shape throughout a tough battle.

In recent years hook manufacturers have tried hard to stay in touch with current trends within carp fishing, one such development being 'the bent hook' (see fig. 3). Originally, a Drennan long-shank carbon lure (trout fishing) hook was bent inwards ¼ in down from the eye. Used in conjunction with a boilie presented on a hair/bolt rig, in consistent hooking terms this format is considered almost flawless. There are now several similar patterns of hooks (already bent) from which to choose, including the Drennan 'starpoint' and the 'Gardner' bent hook. For most situations in carp fishing, however, I still prefer to put my faith in a forged standard round-bend, medium-shank eyed hook whose point has been chemically etched to sharp perfection. I do, however, doctor the barb itself by flattening it with a pair of forceps to aid both penetration and subsequent removal (see fig. 3).

Always check each hook carefully before tying it on, which takes but a second. As with everything man-made, every so often you come across a duff one. In the case of a hook this means that it has not been properly tempered. Test each hook by putting the point beneath your thumb nail and try to lever it open.

For presenting many of the larger particle baits, and especially boilies, to crafty, well-educated carp the bolt rig is extremely effective. This modest-sized common carp accepted a side-hooked black-eyed bean and will come to no harm placed on a foam-lined unhooking mat.

It is often very much easier to unhook carp using long-nosed artery forceps. This young angler has sensibly kept his fish in the wet net and laid it upon a bed of soft grass well away from the gravel margins to remove the hook.

KNOTS

Poorly tied knots, and knots of poor design, are one of the main contributing factors to carp being lost. I still see references in articles and books to the 'five-turn half blood knot' as being a suitable knot for tying eyed hooks to catch big fish like carp. Yet this knot can so easily pull or fracture under the kind of pressures involved.

The knot I put complete faith in is called the mahseer knot, handed on to me by my guide, Suban, when after the legendary fish of that name in India. Its stength (see fig. 4A) lies in the fact that the end is trapped beneath two loops, instead of the standard half blood knots' one loop. For eyed hooks that are going to be used in the most demanding of situations the mahseer knot is unbeatable because it actually 'stretches' under full load instead of strangling the line.

With modern carbon hooks, which have particularly neat eyes, especially in the smaller sizes, the mahseer knot can prove rather bulky to tie. In this case, the seven-turn tucked half blood knot (see fig. 4B) is both quick and easy to tie.

Whilst both these knots are perfect for tying mono-filament, for dacron and other braids the choice lies between two more popular knots. The 'palomar knot' (see fig. 4C) is simple to tie and also creates minimal strangula-tion of the line. It is not an easy knot to manage with small-eyed hooks because the line has to be doubled into a loop and passed through the eye. Devised by the late Richard Walker and named after his son, the 'Grinner' knot (see fig. 4D) is far less constricting than the blood knots and technically more efficient because all five turns around the line are trapped against the eye, not just the end one.

Both of these knots are also good for tying multistrand floss, which is not the easiest material to deal with particularly if you work out of doors and suffer rough finger tips. However, provided you wet the length to be tied and keep it moist whilst bedding the knot down gently, both the palomar and the grinner work efficiently.

While the four previously described knots are all you will ever need for tying hooks and swivels on to the main

FIGURE 4 *Knots*

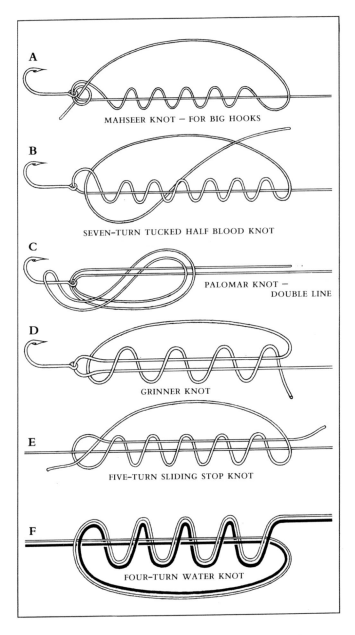

A

MAHSEER KNOT – FOR BIG HOOKS

B

SEVEN-TURN TUCKED HALF BLOOD KNOT

C

PALOMAR KNOT –
DOUBLE LINE

D

GRINNER KNOT

E

FIVE-TURN SLIDING STOP KNOT

F

FOUR-TURN WATER KNOT

line, or for hook and bomb links, etc., to cope with every demand in carp fishing there are two more valuable additions well worth learning to tie. The simple stop knot and the four-turn water knot. The stop knot (see fig. 4E) which can be moved up or down the line (always wet it first) is used in conjunction with a small bead as a stop against which the controller float rests when presenting floating baits. It can be tied with a short length of reel line or power gun which is softer and slides through the rod rings easily. Remember to leave the ends around 1½ in long so they 'fold' when the line passes back and forwards through the rod rings under the pressure of a fish being played.

The four-turn water knot (see fig. 4F) is great for joining a fixed-lead paternoster (of either heavier or lighter strain) to the main line. It has enormous advantages for joining two lines together where the only alternative is a swivel, which all too easily picks up debris and obviously weakens the rig because two extra knots are required. The four-turn water knot is quicker, neater, lighter and most importantly is stronger, because the main line is simply wound around and locked into the added link creating the minimum of constriction.

INDICATORS

Actually watching a carp suck the bait into its huge mouth is, of course, the best bite indication of all. It opens up a fascinating world of knowledge, making carp fun to take from the surface on floaters, especially when they can be observed at close range through really clear water approaching and finally accepting a freelined bait. A line snaking out across the surface is an exciting and most positive indication. In precious few situations (see Free-lining), however, can the line beyond the rod tip be regarded as the indicator to watch.

Coil indicators

Necessity calls for a visual indicator fixed between the butt ring and reel which is easily seen, easily attached, and which relates to both forward and drop-back bites. For years (some still do) anglers simply squeezed a piece of bread or a coil of silver kitchen foil, on to the line midway between butt ring and reel. Simple coil indicators (they can also be made from plastic piping in a variety of weights) are ideal for short freelining or ledgering sessions, especially

FIGURE 5 *Coil*
indicators

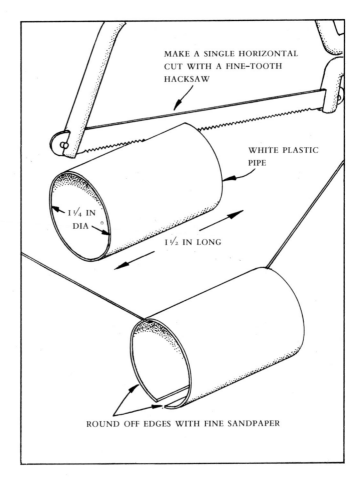

MAKE A SINGLE HORIZONTAL
CUT WITH A FINE–TOOTH
HACKSAW

WHITE PLASTIC
PIPE

I ¼ IN
DIA

I ½ IN LONG

ROUND OFF EDGES WITH FINE SANDPAPER

for the wandering opportunist angler carrying the
minimum of tackle (see fig. 5).

Monkey climbers

The most popular of all carp indicators are, in effect,
'bobbins' on a stick which do not blow about in the wind.
They are available in a variety of weights to counteract
sub-surface tow and to indicate drop-back bites in certain
circumstances. If a certain amount of your carp fishing will
take place during darkness or in poor light, choose a
monkey with a clear body that will accept a luminous
betalight element (see fig. 6). Otherwise, go for bright
daytime colours like yellow or orange. Monkeys which
run super freely on a black (PTFE-coated) stick, aptly

*Having pre-baited a
shallow bar along the
opposite bank, the
angler waits patiently
for a run. The rods are
supported on a 'rod
pod' frame specially
designed for banks of
hard gravel. These
allow the entire set-
up, including bank
sticks, bite alarms and
monkey climbers, to
be moved easily as one
unit.*

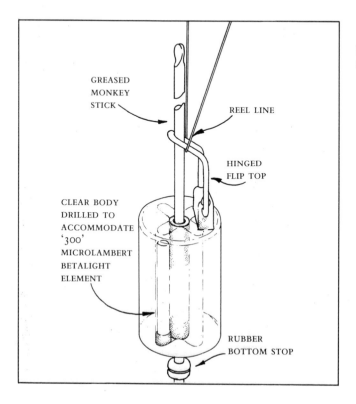

GREASED
MONKEY
STICK

REEL LINE

HINGED
FLIP TOP

CLEAR BODY
DRILLED TO
ACCOMMODATE
'300'
MICROLAMBERT
BETALIGHT
ELEMENT

RUBBER
BOTTOM STOP

Figure 6 *Monkey
climbers*

called 'grease monkeys', are worth the extra money as the body slides up and down effortlessly.

Bite alarms/buzzers

While monkey climbers work perfectly well without any electrical help in registering a bite when ledgering, they are used almost exclusively in conjunction with an electric bite alarm or, as they are affectionately known, a 'buzzer'. Buzzers have now become synonymous with carp fishing almost to the point that some carp fishermen would feel distinctly 'undressed' without them. This is a pity because the substitution of gadgetry for technique rather limits enjoyment.

Antenna-type buzzers

These, the first design in buzzers ever marketed, are still popular because they fit nicely into the lower price bracket and work on the contact-breaker principle. When the line is pulled across the antenna, at the bottom of which is a

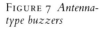

FIGURE 7 *Antenna-type buzzers*

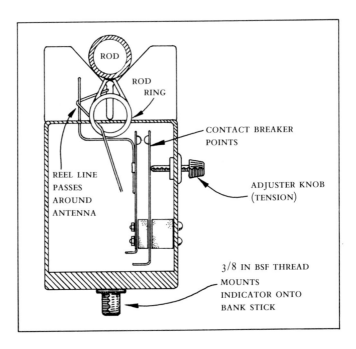

breaker point, contact is made and the buzzer sounds in conjunction with a light-emitting diode for visual warning (see fig. 7).

The antenna can be tensioned or relaxed as required for registering twitches or steady pulls by simple knob adjustment. This type of buzzer, however, is capable of registering only a short or a continuous (so long as the carp keeps swimming away) bite. It cannot relate to the speed at which line is being taken.

Optonic bite indicators

These particular buzzer-alarms, which are in fact now almost standard gear amongst carp enthusiasts, also indicate the speed at which line is being taken off the reel. For every $\frac{1}{4}$ in of line which travels across the sensitive 'wheel' a single bleep tone plus warning light is emitted, so you can instantly relate to the kind of bite, whether it is a mere twitch, a slow run, or a scorching run. As the line rotates the wheel a tiny fan blade spigoted to the wheel with a fine spindle interupts the light beam of a mini photo electric cell.

This system is available in various self-contained cordless compact forms, with or without volume and tone control, and with sensors (or heads) connected by wires to a sounder box which can be positioned several yards away inside a bivi so it effectively becomes an alarm clock. Unfortunately some are even louder than alarm clocks. Another feature available on some models is a green latching light which stays on for 10 seconds (after the bite) to show you on which rod the buzzer indicated should you not have noticed.

The Magnetronic is a new concept from Optonic which looks and works in the same way, but uses a magnet and reed switch in conjunction with the wheel instead of a photo-electric cell. It only drains the standard PP3 battery when the line moves and is noticeably more rain resistant than all previous models.

All electronic bite alarms naturally become the front rod rest heads, for which the 'buzzer bar' was invented. Available in alloy or stainless steel there are buzzer bars to take two, three or even four rods (stick with two) which

Surrounded by the beauty and natural history of a secluded lake, the angler can allow his eyes and mind to wander away from the rods, knowing that the slightest movement of the line will register in a series of bleeps from the Optonic bite indicators.

simply screw into the standard bank-stick thread. For both front and back rests (separate U-type screw-in heads take the rod butts) invest in a pair of telescopic bank sticks to allow for a variety of different marginal levels.

For the really hard banking of some gravel pits, reservoirs and the like, the rod pod is the answer. This is a complete rod set-up with a ground frame combining bank sticks and twin buzzer bars with an aerial bar located in the middle to take monkey climbers. It saves having to crunch about, ramming or hammering in bank sticks which can only distract from the fishing and even spoil the enjoyment and solitude of other anglers close by.

FLOATS

The float of course, is the oldest indicator of them all. And while today's youngsters, through no fault of their own, may well come straight into the carp fishing scene and immediately start to rely on electronic bite alarms coupled

to bolt-rig ledgering set-ups, float fishing will always be available as an art to learn.

There is nothing more exciting than crouching down in the marginal growth holding the rod in anticipation when less than 5 yd out amongst a huge patch of feeding bubbles the float tip suddenly pops upwards and keels right over in a perfect 'lift' bite. Carp do not warrant a super-sensitive range of floats, as do dace or roach. Plain peacock quill cut into suitable lengths, with the herl removed from the stem and the tip painted with ½ in of fluorescent orange or red, is quite adequate. I never bother with eyes or rings at the bottom because threading the line through these could be suicidal should a carp wind its way through heavy weed. In that situation, I want the float to come free instantly, and all I have lost is a few pence. The float is usually fixed at the bottom end only (see 'Float fishing') with a wide section of silicon float rubber. By all means use commercial wagglers or bodied peacock wagglers, but always attach them with silicon tubing as opposed to the eye and 'locking shot' method, because with the list method all shots need to be close to the bait.

For presenting all floating baits, from tiny cat biscuits to a large chunk of bread crust, any further than a few yards, use a loaded floating controller. They are available in a variety of shapes and sizes.

FLOATING CONTROLLERS

Available in all sorts of shapes and sizes, the controller is an indispensible piece of equipment for presenting both small and large floaters to surface-feeding carp. It has a swivel at the top, plus a coloured tip for good visual location at distance, plus a weighted stem so it sits vertically in the surface film.

Controllers originated from the age-old spherical bubble float made from clear plastic, into which water could be put to aid casting. However, striking with bubble floats causes so much water displacement that much of the power never reaches the hook. It was for this reason, unhappy with commercially-produced controllers at that time (now there are several good designs), that I devised my 'Ten-pin' which, as its name implies, is shaped exactly like a bowling pin. Rounded and wide at the top, into which a size 10 Berkeley swivel is glued, it tapers down to a narrow wrist which consists of a weighted stem of brass, plugged into the balsa body. I required a weighted surface controller that could be flipped even underarm from banks suffering badly from overhead branches, up to distances of 30 yd or more. I am pleased to say even the small 'Ten-pin' (there are two sizes) accomplishes this with ease (see Floater fishing).

SUNDRIES

Landing-nets

Traditionally, carp landing-nets have always been tri-angular in shape with two arms supported in a preformed spreader block, fitted with a standard BSF ⅜th thread for screwing into any landing-net pole, whether single stem or telescopic. A nylon cord stretched between the tip of each end keeps them slightly bowed, and thus the whole frame remains reasonably rigid. For several years I have used the North Western specimen net, which has strong, hollow fibre-glass arms and is available in 36 in, 42 in and 50 in sizes. Frankly, having easily slipped two pike each of exactly 50 in long (one a 30-pounder) into the 42 in carp model, I cannot see why anything larger, with its associated awkward manoeuvrability (especially in dense undergrowth), is ever required for carp, taking into account that carp are considerably shorter for their weight than pike.

For 'stalking' carp, I much prefer to carry a smaller net: 24 in diameter, round frame fixed with a 24 in deep twin mesh net, micro at the base with minnow mesh sides. The junction where the screw thread joins the telescopic pole needs to be supported when hoisting out a heavy weight or the frame will collapse, nevertheless this is certainly worth the trouble for the net's portability. I have in fact landed several fish (up to 26¾ lb) with the telescopic pole fully extended and these could not have been netted with a larger, heavier, less manoeuvrable triangle framed net: for example, carp which have become stuck fast on the surface wrapped around lily stems, or which are simply lying there exhausted on the surface immovable in beds of thick soft weeds, tantalizingly beyond the reach of the larger specimen net's single pole. Whichever frame you decide upon (perhaps for overall use, a triangular 36 in model is best) ensure that the net has a micro or soft nylon base (as used in carp sacks) and that the wall mesh is soft and knotless. Twin meshes are extremely popular, and rightly so. The larger wall mesh allows the net to be steered easily through the water, while the soft nylon or micro bottom ensures that the carp's body mucus remains intact and that the terminal rig does not become entangled.

Sacks

If you can take a photo of your carp immediately after capture, it's best not to retain it. Simply leave it in the landing-net (even before unhooking) in the margins while the camera is adjusted and a suitable spot found where the light is even and not full of shadows. Then even self-photography with the aid of an air-release cable can be accomplished quickly and with minimum inconvenience to the carp.

As carp live a long life, and in popular fisheries will no doubt be caught dozens, perhaps even hundreds of times,

For many situations, particularly when stalking modest-sized carp in overgrown waters, a 24 in diameter, round landing-net frame fitted with a deep, twin-mesh net, is infinitely more manouvreable than a giant triangular model. A round net can easily handle fish up to 20 lb.

you owe it to the carp and to the angler after you to return the fish without harm. This entails retaining it in a soft nylon sack of adequate proportions. Sacks punched with numerous holes for the water to pass freely through are highly recommended. They come in various sizes (4 × 5 ft is ideal) with a draw-string top or long zip, and are black in colour which helps keep the carp quiet inside. Remember always to fully soak the sack before putting the carp inside, or some of the carp's valuable body mucus will be removed, leaving it vulnerable to parasites and disease. Select a quiet shaded spot away from full sunlight and tie the retaining cord tightly to a bankside branch. Where none exist, I push my long-nosed forceps into the bank and tie the cord to them. Ensure that the carp has at least 18 in of water so it can fully submerge, and once again retain it for the shortest period of time only. Lastly never put more than one carp into one sack.

Unhooking mats

For the safe removal of hooks – safe that is for the carp, which can all too easily flap up and down on gravel banking and scrape itself raw – unhooking mats have been

designed. For gravel pit fisheries in particular, renowned for stony banks which never grass over, these foam-filled unhooking mats are an absolute must for ensuring that the fish goes back in to the water in the condition it came out. At a pinch, an old square of carpet underlay or piece of ½ in thick dense foam will suffice. Remember, however, to dampen whatever you use so the body mucus is not disturbed.

Weighing carp/slings

Continuing the theme of disturbing the fish's condition as little as possible, it's just as easy to unscrew the landing-net top and hoist it on to the scales complete with carp to weigh it, remembering to deduct the net's weight afterwards, as to remove the carp to weigh it. Should this prove impossible, have a large pre-wetted, soft nylon sling handy into which the carp can be gently moved immediately after unhooking. After weighing, take the sling into the water and allow the carp to swim out under its own steam. This is also a good time for that final 'returning' photo.

CHAPTER FIVE

BAITS

FROM the vast majority of what is written today about carp baits the newcomer could easily be led into thinking that only designer boilies concocted from a high nutritional value protein mix and flavoured with exotic essences or oils from the far east will catch carp. This, of course, is not true.

Carp derive nutritional value from almost any food source and can be caught on a whole variety of baits, not just boilies. In fact I cannot think of any bait apart from a spinner (even these account for the odd carp) which carp will not readily accept.

What must be accepted, however, is that the more times they are caught on a particular kind, type, flavour, shape or even size of bait, the more suspicious they naturally become. So that, and this applies especially to carp in hard-fished waters, eventually they learn to refuse all the more commonly used baits that have fooled them in the past – baits like bread in all its forms, sweetcorn, luncheon meat, simple pastes and so on. The answer is to find new baits that they will eagerly accept. To stay catching, you need to be forever ringing the changes, switching from one bait to another once the bulk of the carp you are after start to wise up. It is always worthwhile baiting up with a new offering whilst still catching them with the old bait, before its effectiveness wears out.

All this is not to say that even carp from waters where they have seen every bait before will not accept a much used bait under the right circumstances, presented either differently or in a spot the carp have never learnt to associate with danger. The record carp of 51 lb 6 oz caught by Chris Yates from famous Redmire pool in 1980, for instance, sucked up what was then a much used bait, namely sweetcorn. And more than any other fishery in the country, Redmire's carp have seen every new bait ever invented, but this did not stop Chris using sweetcorn effectively, presented beneath a float, too. The secret is to

Manufactured carp baits have certainly come a long way. The prepacked ingredients available from most specialist tackle shops allow you to enjoy an absorbing side hobby by concocting your own designer baits.

keep an open mind on the subject of bait and through observation, trial and error, combined with the experiences of other anglers fishing the same water, try various types of bait until runs occur on a regular basis. Do not ever run away with the idea that there is a magic bait, one to catch carp from wherever you fish, because such a bait doesn't exist.

Learn to use a whole variety of baits, and experience will teach you where each is applicable. Don't sit there with a lump of bread flake on the hook when all the carp in the lake grew wise to bread and lost their interest in it 10 years ago. Several sessions using a particular bait without a run should help the penny drop. By the same token, don't go in with a 12-bore to shoot a sparrow. In other words don't spend a fortune on the latest-flavoured boilies to catch carp which have only recently been introduced into a lake, or have seen little prior attention from anglers. In both cases, it's well worth keeping something in reserve while experimenting with far cheaper and more commonly used baits.

This is not a cookery book, and you will not find a whole list of recipes for making different-flavoured and

different-structured boilies, as good and effective a bait as they are. And make no mistake about it, boilies are a fine bait – the most effective carp bait ever devised. However, the boilie is just one type of bait amongst dozens. Besides, tackle shops sell a wide enough choice of manufactured boiled baits, in terms of colour, size and flavours, shelf life and frozen, without my repeating them all. I am going to take you back through the history of carp fishing baits by providing a comprehensive list of exactly what can be used to catch carp.

Don't just stick to luncheon meat. The variety of tinned and sausage type meats available from the local delicatessen or supermarket is enormous. They can be cut into oblongs or cubes with a thin, long-bladed knife.

MANUFACTURED BAITS

Bread

Bread can be used in several ways, either new, as '*flake*' compressed onto the hook, *crust* fished on the surface, or the inside of the loaf (one several days old is best) kneaded with water into a *paste*. To this paste various flavourings and colourings may be added: *custard powder* which turns it yellow; *aniseed* which really makes it smell; *marmite* or *Bovril* to give it a savoury smell; *grated cheese* to pep it up (a great chub and barbel bait this); and so on. Bread has many possibilities. I once asked a friend who is a baker to bake me half a dozen loaves dyed black with powder colouring, because the carp I was after at the time were scared by the whiteness of ordinary bread. And very effective the *black flake* and *black crusts* proved too. Plain white flake, however, is one of the best crucian baits around.

Cheese

Cut into *small cubes* cheese can be fished on a hair rig (see 'Ledgering' p. 116), or simply freelined (p. 88), float-fished (p. 91), or presented on a standard ledger rig (p. 112). There are countless textures and flavours to try. Plain ordinary *processed cheese* sold from large blocks is probably the nicest to use. The smelly, crumbly ones, like *Danish Blue* or *Gorgonzola* are best mixed into a stiff paste with equal quantities of bread paste. There is lots to experiment with here.

Meats

A tin of *luncheon meat* should always be kept in the back of the car or in the tackle bag as a standby. It is a sound investment. Cut into cubes (no longer than the hook shank) luncheon meat will catch carp from anywhere. *Stuffed pork roll*, tinned *ham*, and *spam* are also worth trying. Or what about all those spicey sausages in skins like *garlic sausage*, or *black pudding* made largely from pigs' blood; they are all fabulous carp attractors which, when cut into cubes, offer an endless variety of baits. The trouble is that you can't stop eating them, as all luncheon meat fans know only too well. Fresh meats are effective too, especially *liver*, either pigs' or calves' liver, carefully cut into squares and used like luncheon meat straight on the hook, or on a hair rig (p. 116). *Raw steak* shares with liver a high blood content which is particularly attractive to carp. It too should be cut into squares with a sharp knife, and, because of its stringy consistency, presented on a hair.

Tinned sausages like chipolatas cut into segments make great baits, as do both *pork* or *beef sausages* that have been cooked and left to cool, because then they can be cut into squares or oblongs.

Pork or beef *sausage meat* makes a fine paste. Simply keep adding flour whilst kneading until the stickiness disappears, leaving a firm hook bait which can be easily moulded.

Liver sausage, although expensive, kneads into a lovely smooth paste with cornflour added to stiffen it. Add a drop or two of brown liquid colouring if you think it is too light.

Tinned cat foods are available in dozens of different flavours which potentially all make excellent paste baits. Stiffen with cornflour and some wheatgerm until firm enough, and then test in a glass of water to see how long it will last without disintegrating. Add a small quantity of wheat gluten to act as a binder in brands which are difficult to work with.

PELLET FEED

By far the most effective bait available in pellet form – manufactured in various sizes from fry crumb to ½ in diameter holding pellets – are those produced for the sole purpose of rearing trout and salmon. Formulated in various proportions of fish meal, oils and binders, *trout pellets* are effective as a surface attractor in their floating form, and as a sinking loose-feed crumb in the smallest sinking size. *Salmon fry crumb*, which have a higher oily fish content and are much darker in colour are especially good.

To convert this effective bait into a paste, put into a bowl and wet (without oversoaking) with hot water. Leave for 30 minutes to allow all the water to be absorbed, and then knead into a stiff paste adding cornflour to blot up any excess water. For added attraction (although these pellets are a complete food in themselves) Bovril, marmite, or Phillips yeast mixture (a bird tonic) may be mixed into the paste, which can then be popped into a polybag and put in the freezer for later use.

Pig pellets may also be kneaded into an aromatic paste to

good effect by following the same procedure. In fact all animal pellet food is worth experimenting with as potential carp baits. Those which do not hold together well are improved with the addition of beaten eggs to bind the mixture together plus cornflour or wheat gluten to stiffen it.

DRIED MILK PASTES

Coloured pastes with a rubbery texture guaranteed to withstand the attentions of small, nuisance species, are easily made from a mixture of dried milk derivatives, wheatgerm, flavouring and powder dye mixed with water.

Some of the richest derivatives to be extracted from milk make very effective paste baits. There are so many recipes this book could not contain them all, so here is a basic formula. Mix dry in a bowl one part of Casilan (from chemists) or calcium calcinate to two parts of Beemax (also from chemists) or plain wheatgerm. Then add sufficient water to which liquid or powder colour, plus a flavour, has been added and knead into a soft paste. The resulting paste will be rather sticky and rubbery, which makes it almost impervious to the pecking attentions of small unwanted nuisance species. Contrary to popular belief, this bait can be frozen for later use.

PARTICLE BAITS

These work effectively because much of the carp's natural daily diet consists of tiny particles of food sucked up individually over a wide area (see 'Feeding') as opposed to large concentrated food items.

Hempseed is the most effective particle of all, especially as an attractor because it really gets carp rooting about and holds them within a given area. Though it is individually too small to put on to a carp hook it can be threaded on to a fine hair stringer and tied in at the eye of the hook (fig. 8). Alternatively, and this is my preference, simply pre-bait or loose feed with stewed hempseed and on the hook use a larger particle. I once thought that only other small, darkish seeds or peas really worked in conjunction with hemp and in certain situations this still holds true, but when carp are really going potty on hempseed and chewing the bottom up, almost anything on the hook will produce a bite.

Dari seed is another small seed which like hemp is a fine attractor and is best presented several seeds at a time on a hair stringer (fig. 8).

The colourful array of baits shown here, most of which are available either pre-cooked in tins or in dried form, represent just a small selection of the particle baits which will catch carp. Use your imagination.

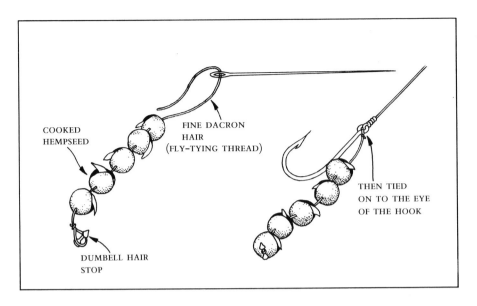

COOKED
HEMPSEED

FINE DACRON
HAIR
(FLY–TYING THREAD)

THEN TIED
ON TO THE EYE
OF THE HOOK

DUMBELL HAIR
STOP

FIGURE 8 *Threading hempseed onto a hair stringer*

Maple peas are an excellent hook bait used together with attractors like hemp, tares, or daris, or simply by itself as bait and attractor.

Tic beans are not unlike maples but are larger, heavier and work in the same way. They are a much under-rated carp bait.

Tares are only slightly larger than hemp (after stewing). They work effectively as both hook bait (on a hair stringer, fig. 8) and smelly attractors if left to stew in their own juices for a few days.

Wheat, once stewed, has a lovely nutty smell and is a really effective yet seldom-used, inexpensive particle bait. It is large enough to be fished two up on the hook, or threaded on to a hair. When its effectiveness starts to wane it can even be coloured by adding powder dye to the stewing water. Red and orange are favourites. The addition of a flavour might also help – try aniseed.

Maize needs to be pre-soaked for two days in hot water and then pressure cooked for 20 minutes, otherwise it appears too hard to use as bait. The prepared grain swells to twice its size, not unlike a giant but brighter grain of wheat (one grain to a size 8 hook is ideal). It is always much harder than wheat, however, and thus impervious to the attentions of small fish. Like wheat, it too may be coloured and flavoured although part of its secret is, I am sure, the pungent, nutty smell.

Sweetcorn is probably the most successful particle bait of all time, though its effectiveness soon wears off when everybody starts using it. It is, of course, a hybrid of the maize plant. Harvested while still soft, young and sweet, and not left to dry on the cob, its life may be extended as a bait on waters where carp have become suspicious of this 'yellow peril' by dyeing it with a powder colour mixed into a little hot water. Bright red or purple sweetcorn looks terrific and catches well. It is always worth keeping a tin or two in the tackle bag or boot of the car for catching crucian carp alone.

Peanuts are much loved by carp, and providing they are prepared properly will, contrary to popular belief, do the fish no harm. Put them into a tub with a rip-off lid, with plenty of space to spare. Cover by at least several inches of boiling water, to allow the nuts to expand fully. Fix the lid on tightly and leave for two days. Drain the excess water off and the nuts are ready for immediate use – or pop into polybags and into the freezer.

Standard-sized, ready-shelled nuts may be purchased reasonably cheaply from pet shops by the lb or in bulk. These are ideal for pre-baiting and loose feed. The much larger (and more expensive) jumbo-sized American peanuts make fabulous hook baits, one being nicely matched to a size 6 or 4 hook, and nicked on gently (side hooked) through either end leaving the point and barb well exposed. Two nuts are best threaded on to a hair.

Possessing tremendous inherent buoyancy, peanuts are great for fishing over and into thick weed. They tend to rest on top and remain visible to patrolling carp, unlike heavier particles which fall through and become hidden. Used over a bed of hempseed, American peanuts are a deadly bait whether float-fished (p. 91) or ledgered on a bolt rig (p. 117).

You must prepare *tiger nuts* in exactly the same way as maize or they cannot be used as bait. They are in fact a vegetarian food (available from health food shops) with a delightful crunchy, nutty flavour, for which carp also share a liking. To get carp really on to tigers may take several pre-baiting sessions, but once they have learnt to appreciate them, expect some fast action. Like peanuts they stay on well, and so can be reliably cast long distances. Tigers are also a great marginal bait. I present

To prepare extremely hard particles for carp baits, such as maize or the tiger nuts shown here, pre-soak for 2 days in cold water prior to pressure cooking for 20 minutes.

them two up on a size 4 hook beneath a length of peacock quill lift style (p. 94).

Black eyed beans are a rather bland salad bean. With its distinctive black eye, it catches well and is most versatile. It is cheap to buy in dry form from health food shops (or in tins already cooked), and may be prepared to your (or the carp's) liking. Stew as for peanuts adding colour and flavour as required. My favourite colours are dark red, brown, or orange, flavoured with caramel or butterscotch, but of course the permutations are endless. Present one on a size 8, two on a size 4 directly on to the hook, leaving the point and barb clear or thread on to a hair (fig. 8).

Chick peas. This round salad favourite, another excellent alternative for ringing the changes, is prepared, coloured and flavoured in exactly the same way as black eyes, or purchased pre-cooked in tins.

Butter beans. These flattish beans, largest by far of the particles, are tailor-made for fishing over dense weed-beds or thick silt. They are available uncoloured and pre-cooked in tins or may be purchased dry and then stewed, coloured and flavoured as all the other beans. Their size obviously permits the use of large hooks and even a single butter bean is heavy enough to freeline (p. 88) provided you cast gently.

Red kidney beans. If like me you adore 'Chili con carne', then this large, dark purple bean is no stranger. Carp love them too, whether presented over a bed of smaller attractors such as hemp or tares, or just as they are. As they need neither colour nor flavouring, simply buy them pre-cooked in tins and strain off the juices. Hook sizes 6 to 4 are ideal. To economize for regular pre-baiting, they can be purchased in bulk from health food shops and prepared in the same way as peanuts. Never be tempted to chew these beans unless they have been well stewed.

Borlotti beans also have the convenience of being available ready-cooked in a tin. Dark red in colour and slightly larger than a baked bean, individual beans should be side-hooked on a size 8 hook or presented on a hair two or even three up. Loose feed and pre-bait with the same, or use over an attractor such as hempseed.

Haricot beans. This, the most consumed bean of all when cooked in tomato sauce, is another 'change' particle bait. Buy tins of baked beans and drain off the sauce if you prefer them ready coloured, or buy a tin of plain haricot beans. One on a size 10 or two on an 8 does nicely.

NATURALS

Large quantities of stretched, dead maggots are sometimes the unfortunate result of heatwave conditions, when the tackle dealers' refrigeration units cannot cope with the warmth that the maggots generate. However, they can be put to good use for pre-baiting, and quickly turn carp into a feeding frenzy.

Maggots

These are without question as effective for catching carp (including crucians) as they are for most other species. And in the vast majority of fisheries this is the problem – maggots are not selective enough. Everything from a plump gudgeon upwards has not the slightest problem with even four maggots on a size 10 hook. There are two ways of dealing with this problem. Use maggots only in waters where carp are the dominant species. Or put so many in that when the nuisance fish become full up the carp move in and start pulling the bottom apart. Funnily enough, such a feeding pattern is induced whenever the fridge packs up in my tackle shop (usually in heatwave conditions), because dozens of gallons of 'stretched' maggots get tossed into the carp lake nearest the house. And wherever that spot happens to be, within an hour or two it is turned into a churning, bubbling, muddy mass of carp feeding with real abandon, their tails wavering across the surface as they skim along on their noses hoovering up the sudden food mass.

FIGURE 9 *Hair-rigged casters*

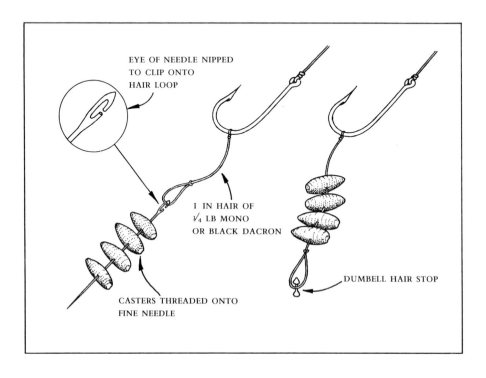

EYE OF NEEDLE NIPPED TO CLIP ONTO HAIR LOOP

1 IN HAIR OF ¼ LB MONO OR BLACK DACRON

CASTERS THREADED ONTO FINE NEEDLE

DUMBELL HAIR STOP

Casters

Casters share the same pulling power as maggots for both nuisance species and carp, with the added benefit that they do not burrow into the silt or dense weed and become invisible. So in effect you need far less for loose feed. Carp also love floating casters, but to present them delicately without numerous refusals unusually light terminal tackle needs to be employed. Alternatively, they can be presented on a long hair, two, three or four up (fig. 9).

Worms

With the availability nowadays of so many manufactured baits, the poor old *worm* does not rate much of a look in. Considering that worms are free, this is a great pity because they are extremely effective carp baits. Use brandlings individually topped with a grain of corn, or two brandlings on a size 12 for crucian carp.

Larger carp always accept bunches of brandlings readily,

FIGURE 10 *Air-injected lobworm*

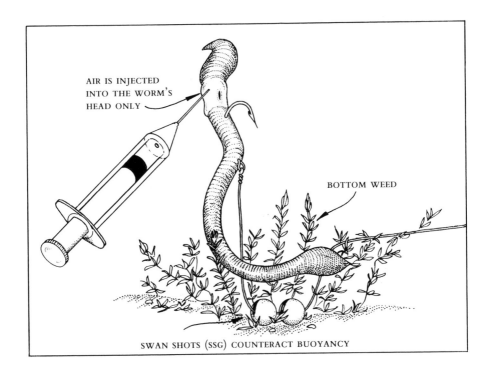

AIR IS INJECTED INTO THE WORM'S HEAD ONLY

BOTTOM WEED

SWAN SHOTS (SSG) COUNTERACT BUOYANCY

especially when they are rooting in silt and preoccupied with blood worms, while a large gyrating lobworm brings out that natural, animal aggression. Simply freeline (p. 88) on a size 6, or present beneath a float (p. 91), laid well on the bottom with a single shot 10 in from the hook. In really thick bottom weed, inject the head of the lob with a little air from a hypodermic syringe so it floats tantalizingly above the weed, using a swan shot or two to compensate for its buoyancy (fig. 10).

Shrimps/prawns

The most convenient way of buying these super baits is ready boiled, peeled and frozen from the local super-market. They may also be coloured. However, owing to their natural shellfish flavour, offering them just as they are usually produces action, even from particularly difficult carp. Pre-baiting works wonders, using at least 1 pint for every session.

Cockles

Cockles are also best purchased having been first boiled and de-shelled. Fishmongers sell them in bulk, enabling a batch to be split up into several polybags and popped into the freezer for later use. As with prawns, pre-baiting produces the goods and this necessitates introducing 1 pint or so into the swim for several consecutive days before actually fishing. Due to their bland taste, cockles are ideal for experimenting with flavours. Have a go at colouring them too. Use bright pink, red or orange powder dye – the results are staggering.

Mussels

Generally speaking freshwater mussels, and in particular the largest – the well-known swan mussel – seem to grow best of all in rich silty waters, be they estate lakes, ponds or pits. They can easily be gathered by pulling a long-handled garden rake along the bottom of the margins, and kept in a

An old-hat bait it may well be, and like as not most modern carp fishermen will probably not have used the succulent orange meat found in-side the swan mussel. However it's free, it can be gathered from the lake margins, and is a part of the carp's natural diet.

bucket of water for a few days. To open the clam-like shell, use a thin-bladed knife to sever the powerful hinges holding the two halves together. This reveals the orange meat inside – a food source which carp almost everywhere will relish. A large chunk on a size 2 or 4 hook provides a fabulous bait, while the leftovers plus the insides from several other large mussels provides an attractive ground bait. Pre-baiting a swim every other day with the insides of 20 swan mussels could well provoke even difficult, well-fished carp that have seen all the regular pre-made baits, into a feeding frenzy. Try it and see. You do not need to use heavy leads or a bolt-rig set up for this approach. All you need to do is freeline (p. 88) the mussel meat and wait for the line to start peeling steadily from the spool in a confident run.

FLOATERS

Breadcrust

On heavily fished waters floating crust is considered to be very old hat, and thus an ineffective bait for carp. Nevertheless, it still has pulling power and will catch in new fisheries and in fast, well-stocked carp waters where competition for food among the fish is always high. Use the tough crusts cut from either a white tin loaf or French bread.

Pedigree chum mixers

These, the most popular and certainly the most versatile of floating carp baits, can also be coloured and flavoured in addition to using them straight from the box. Being small and square, they catapult well, are relatively cheap if purchased in bulk (3.5 kg bags), and fairly impervious to the attentions of small nuisance fish. To prepare mixers for hooking, hold a double handful under the tap so they are all wet and pop straight into a polybag. Twenty minutes later they will have absorbed the moisture, and will be easy to hook without disintegrating whether you side-hook one, or thread two or three on to a floating hair rig (see 'Floater fishing', p. 101).

My favourite way of 'doctoring' mixers is to gently heat a batch for a couple of minutes in a frying pan containing a liberal covering of garlic butter. And there are countless permutations for spicing them up once carp noticeably become suspicious of them in their plain form. Experiment and have some fun.

Cat biscuits

Cat biscuits also make wonderful floaters for carp. They come in all sorts of shapes too, ovals, stars, rounds, even mini fish shapes. Pet food supply stores offer them in bulk in both meat and fishy flavours. Prepare in exactly the same way as 'mixers' for easy hooking.

Sunflower seeds

Sunflower seeds, which require soaking for a few hours for ease of hooking, are perhaps an unusual but nonetheless effective floater, possibly due to their high oil content. Whenever I sweep out the cockatiel aviary and dump the entire mess of loose seeds on to the surface of the lake closest to the house, the carp are up on the top and mopping them up post haste. Only soak those required for hook baits.

Boilies

Floating boilies are a bait which small, unwanted species like rudd and roach cannot peck to bits, and as such are the most selective of all floaters, whether side-hooked or presented on a hair.

Offer just one large (18–20 mm) boilie, which really stands out amongst a scattering of small attractor floaters such as cat biscuits or chum mixers; or a floating boilie of any size amongst a small scattering of others of the identical colour and size (see 'Floater fishing', p. 101).

If you cannot find pre-made floaters in the tackle shop of the size, colour and flavour desired, simply put a batch of regular, sinking boilies into a shallow baking tray and pop into a pre-heated oven for a few minutes. They should all then float. Experiment to make perfect.

BOILED BAITS (BOILIES)

I have purposefully left boiled baits, or 'boilies' as they are affectionately known, until the end of this chapter. They are not the panacea for catching carp easily that certain bait manufacturers would have us believe. However, boilies are extremely effective, and are a most selective bait for carp because nuisance species cannot deal with them. Either their pharyngeal teeth are not powerful enough to crush the outer skin enabling the soft insides to be swallowed (which is the whole idea of wrapping a

Baits for catching carp off the surface are cheap, readily available and easily catapulted.

protective skin around the bait), or their mouths are simply too small.

It is said that there is nothing new in fishing and at times this fact is really brought home. For instance, one of the most famous carp baits of yesteryear, though seldom used nowadays – par-boiled potatoes – was in reality nothing less than a boilie years ahead of its time. But then, huge paste baits made from millet flour and boiled to enhance the natural gluten so as to make the surface rubbery and thus impervious to unwanted species, were concocted in India at least 100 years ago by those who sought the legendary mahseer. And now anyone can walk into even a non-specialist tackle shop and be spoilt for choice by the sheer amount of varying sizes, colours and flavours of boiled baits on offer, both frozen and shelf life.

Shelf-life boilies are certainly the most convenient of manufactured baits. You simply need to choose a size from minis up to gob-stopper, 20 mm ones, select a flavour and colour which hasn't seen much use on the water in question, and give them a try. There is no wonder flavour or magic boilie, so don't waste your time looking for one.

Consider (and ask the salesman about) the bait's density

and whether it will lie lightly on top of weed or fall
through. Think about various colours and how they will
relate to the colour of the bottom the bait is presented
over. Will they blend in naturally or stand out. Think
about the flavour. Do you want one which is used
regularly on the water you fish because the carp have
become accustomed to it, but also possibly scared by it
through being caught too many times? Or is an entirely
new and unknown flavour more likely to score once
several pre-baiting sessions have accustomed the carp to a
different food source?

These are the questions you should consider when
purchasing pre-made boilies, and if you are not entirely
happy then simply make you own. Bait suppliers not only
provide all the component parts, they also give suggested
recipes.

A comparatively new invention in the history of carp baits, and marketed only since the 1980s, ready-made boilies are available in a staggering variety of colours, flavours and sizes.

CHAPTER SIX

TECHNIQUES AND RIGS

FREELINING

If you spend any time at all observing carp and how they relate to a baited hook, you will soon understand why the simple method of freelining the bait without any foreign bits on the line (floats, shots, bombs, tubing, etc), other than the hook, is the most sensitive method of all. Unless the carp picks up the line with its large pectoral or pelvic fins, or brushes up against it and does a runner, it will trundle confidently off with the bait as though your hook did not exist.

To freeline any further out than a few yards, the bait needs to be reasonably heavy; the insides of a swan mussel, a cube of meat, a large lump of paste or bread flake, a 20 mm boilie and so on. In all cases, the hook by comparison weighs next to nothing. So unless the carp is aware of your presence, or is wary of the bait itself in which case it might quickly snatch and blow it out with equal speed (sometimes a quick strike when watching this happen will score), a confident bite usually occurs. If you cannot see the bait being taken, which is probably the case more often than not, keep your eyes glued to the line. Never be tempted to straighten the way in which it hangs between the rod tip and surface in a gentle bow, or how it lies loosely on the surface, because this in effect is your bite indicator.

When the line twitches (as the carp sucks in the bait), and then starts to straighten or simply tightens across the surface without any prior warning, there is no finer or more positive indication of a confident bite. Whenever carp are in the immediate area and might literally pick the bait up at any second, I rarely put the rod down. If, however, a long wait seems imminent the rod may be carefully laid on marginal plants with an ever-watchful eye kept on the line, or put in two rests with the tip pointed at the bait.

If, due to light patterns, dense undergrowth and so on, the line beyond the rod tip cannot be easily seen, use a light, simple, bobbin indicator on the line between reel and butt ring. A coil of silver foil (see 'Indicators' p. 57) is perfect because an exciting 'rustle' is often heard as the foil lifts upwards when the line tightens. At a pinch, squeeze a piece of bread on the line. When a carp takes the bait and moves towards the rod the line usually falls slack. These 'dropbacks' are in fact just as confident as 'forward' runs and should be struck immediately.

In lakes or pits with uneven bottoms where the line between bait and rod tip may come to rest amongst a patch of soft weed or between the stones on a gravel bar, dropback bites do not always register. For this reason, and because distance is anyway restricted as only the bait provides weight for casting, the method of freelining should be considered a technique for close-range fishing, say distances of up to no more than 25–30 yd.

I find freelining most effective for carp inhabiting smallish, weedy overgrown lakes and pits where casting with float or ledger tackle is particularly awkward. At spots that are too limited in marginal space for setting up rod rests and so on, freelining can be a very mobile technique. You can keep on the move seeking new swims, plopping the bait into all the promising-looking areas and resting the bait on the bottom for a minute or so before recasting to each new spot. In high summer, early in the morning or at dusk when carp are most likely to be continually on the move, sport can sometimes even prove instant. Watch the line from the moment the bait hits the surface for those aggressive and sudden takes on the drop, when from nothing the line tightens at speed.

Don't be afraid to be continually casting – there are times when impatience is just as important as patience. Try not to plop a bait directly above a patrolling group of carp. Place it well to the side so its entry will not scare them but its slow free fall to the bottom will not go unnoticed, perhaps tempting one of them to intercept it. Freelined baits may even be cast directly into weed beds such as lilies, because there is nothing to get caught on them. Its simplicity is its secret.

There is no one particular bait which works best when freelined, but in terms of preference I would rate heavy naturals like mussels, a bunch of cockles, a large cube of meat or large lobworms as the best for presenting on the bottom. Slow-sinking (flattened) pieces of paste (trout pellet paste) or breadflake encourage bites on the drop.

Opposite: Freeline tactics used in conjunction with an electric indicator, with the bait placed close in alongside the beds of marginal rushes, accounted for this lively, early morning carp.

FLOAT FISHING

The vast majority of experienced anglers would recognize float fishing as the most sensitive and effective method of presentation because the fish (whatever the species) feels the absolute minimum of resistance when it sucks in the bait and pulls the float under. Yet these same anglers share a mental blockage when contemplating catching carp on

Not all specimen carp are taken by ledgering high-protein boilies at long range. John took this superb leather carp on float-fished peanuts directly beneath the rod tip in just 3 ft of water. Even to get within casting distance of such fish, the prerequisites are stealth and observation.

float tackle. Why? I only wish I knew, because the plain truth is that carp are no different from any other species and fall readily to all float-fishing techniques.

It is true to say of course that big, old, crafty carp living in crystal-clear water are often scared by a vertical line stretched between the float and the bottom shots. But then, they are also scared by a ledgered line set horizontally anywhere from 1 in to 2 ft above the bottom, especially those wound up tight as a bow string, because in their world nothing beneath the surface is ever that rigid. All sub-surface plants bend to their bodies as they pass between the stems, which is why carp are quick to panic off, giving those sudden eruptions in shallow water that we call 'liners', when they bump into a tight line.

There are plus and minus points for each and every technique. However, let me seriously suggest that, armed with a selection of varying float rigs, you will be far better equipped to tackle carp wherever they live than you will be with the knowledge of just one modern-day ledgering rig such as the bolt rig (which is the case with so many of today's carp enthusiasts, who only ever associate catching the species with heavy lead rigs [see 'Ledgering', p. 112]).

Simple float rig

To start with, let's consider a simple float rig for offering a bait close into really shallow, possibly heavily reeded, margins where ledgering might easily spook patrolling carp. Even if the sound waves of a heavy lead going in doesn't scare them, the line stretched 'hauser' fashion from bait to rod tip most certainly will. They simply fade away when they sense the line or bump accidentally into it, and promptly vacate the area in blind panic. Neither occurrence is conducive to seeing a fat carp in the bottom of the net, and to overcome this consider the float rig in fig. 11 designed for *Laying on*. Simply attach 1 in of peacock quill (a tiny waggler will do nicely) to the line with a silicone rubber band at each end. After tying on the hook, set the float well overdepth so that at least 3 ft of line lies along the bottom. Then fix on a small shot (a no. 1) below the float, slightly deeper than the swim. The rod may then be placed in two rests or held.

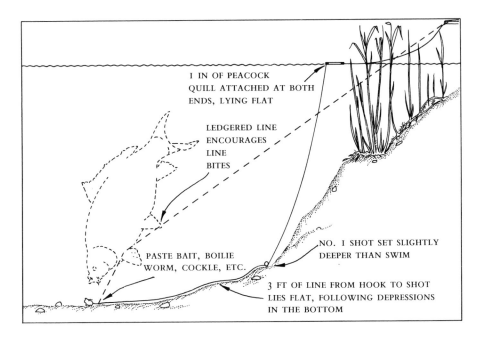

I IN OF PEACOCK
QUILL ATTACHED AT BOTH
ENDS, LYING FLAT

LEDGERED LINE
ENCOURAGES
LINE
BITES

PASTE BAIT, BOILIE
WORM, COCKLE, ETC.

NO. I SHOT SET SLIGHTLY
DEEPER THAN SWIM

3 FT OF LINE FROM HOOK TO SHOT
LIES FLAT, FOLLOWING DEPRESSIONS
IN THE BOTTOM

The point of not having the float cocked is that water displacement caused by a carp's tail could move the line and dip the float momentarily (the float sometimes 'twitches' when fish are in the swim) and entice you into striking when there is no bite. When a carp does move off with the bait there is absolutely no messing. The float positively sinks from view as the line from bait to rod tip straightens.

FIGURE 11 *Laying on*

Lift rigs

For fishing deeper swims over gravel ledges, immediately over or between beds of lilies, potomogeton, dwarf pond lily or amphibious bistort, increase the peacock stem to 2 in long and fix the bottom end only to create a *mini lift rig* (fig. 12). Pinch a swan shot on lightly (so it comes off easily if the fish ploughs through weed) 3 in from the hook and set the float slightly overdepth so it cocks easily when you tighten up. I find that it is imperative to hold the rod in order to use the 'mini lift' effectively. Sometimes bites consist of a gentle, mere 'lifting' or slow 'sinking' of the quill, seemingly not the kind of bite associated with a double-figure carp. But, and this is what float fishing as

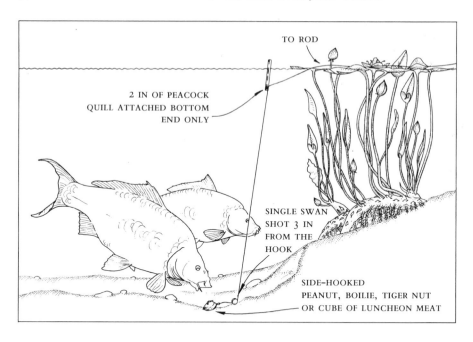

TO ROD

2 IN OF PEACOCK
QUILL ATTACHED BOTTOM
END ONLY

SINGLE SWAN
SHOT 3 IN
FROM THE
HOOK

SIDE-HOOKED
PEANUT, BOILIE, TIGER NUT
OR CUBE OF LUNCHEON MEAT

FIGURE 12 *Mini lift rig*

opposed to ledgering quickly teaches you, carp much of the time bite very delicately indeed because they are deliberate in their movements. It really depends on their mood at the time, because on occasions the float will just carry on going with such speed the fish does in fact hook itself. The 'mini lift' works wonderfully when presenting side-hooked particles or cubes of meat, etc. over loose-feed attractors like hempseed or tares.

Carp bubbling contentedly in the margins between beds of lilies are not too happy about a 2 oz lead landing amongst them. This is where float-fishing techniques, and in particular the lift method, are so effective. Very often a bait can be accurately placed and a carp hooked in less time than it has taken to write this.

Youngsters especially love the intrigue and visual excitement of float fishing for carp. They catch quality fish, too, as young Jonathan Ross proved with this superb 15 lb common, beaten on just 6 lb test.

For presenting the bait accurately, yet at a reasonable distance out from the margins where carp are bubbling away in coloured water over loose feed or alongside lilies, increase the quill length to at least 6 in and pinch on two swan shots 4 in from the hook. With the *lift rig* (fig. 13) bites will now register in an unbelievably positive way, the buoyant quill rising quickly above the surface and keeling right over. Or the float tip will perhaps 'dither' for a second or two (as the carp blows the bait in and out) before vanishing completely. Either way, an instant strike is imperative so don't be tempted to put the rod down. Modern carp rods are very light, and besides, you would not think twice about holding a 13 ft trotting rod to fish a river for several hours, so why not hold the carp rod too. Actually holding the rod stops you getting lazy, always a danger in carp fishing when the action is slow, and keeps

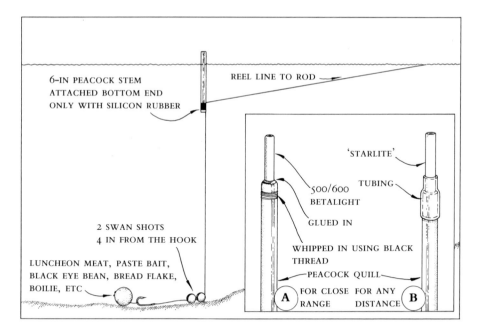

6-IN PEACOCK STEM
ATTACHED BOTTOM END
ONLY WITH SILICON RUBBER

REEL LINE TO ROD

'STARLITE'

500/600
BETALIGHT

TUBING

GLUED IN

2 SWAN SHOTS
4 IN FROM THE HOOK

WHIPPED IN USING BLACK
THREAD

LUNCHEON MEAT, PASTE BAIT,
BLACK EYE BEAN, BREAD FLAKE,
BOILIE, ETC

PEACOCK QUILL

A FOR CLOSE
RANGE

FOR ANY
DISTANCE B

FIGURES 13 AND 14
13 *Lift rig* and 14 *Lift float fishing at night*

your mind alert. It makes you impatient for a bite, which is a good thing because opportune carp are the essence of float fishing.

Lift float fishing at night

Carp which inhabit very clear waters, or lakes and pits where marginal cover is sparse, are more inclined to feed close into the bank under the cloak of darkness. They then become nicely catchable with the lift method. Use a peacock quill fitted with a luminous element so that you can see the float easily.

For fishing close in just beyond the rod tip, and regular sessions at night, it pays to invest in a 500/600 micro-lambert (the most powerful) betalight luminous element, which is easily glued and whipped into the top of a peacock stem (fig. 14).

For the occasional night trip, and for fishing out well beyond the rod tip, use a 'standard' luminous 'starlite' chemical element which is very bright but lasts only for eight hours. It is easily slipped on to the tip of the peacock quill with a short length of clear tubing which comes supplied with the element.

Hair rigs

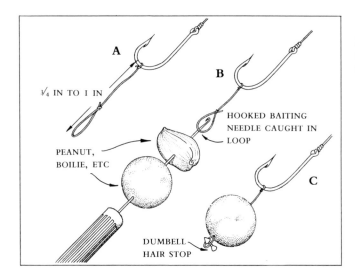

A

B

¼ IN TO 1 IN

HOOKED BAITING
NEEDLE CAUGHT IN
LOOP

PEANUT,
BOILIE, ETC

C

DUMBELL
HAIR STOP

FIGURE 15 *Adding
hair to hook (on lift
rig)*

Returning to daytime fishing again, when bites are not
forthcoming on the lift rig, but fish are obviously in the
swim attracted by the loose feed, you can make the hook
bait more appealing and easier to suck up without the carp
feeling the initial weight and presence of the hook by
threading the bait on to a 'hair'. Though developed for
ledger rigs, the 'hair' works perfectly well when float
fishing, whatever the technique. It is simply a short length
of fine (¾ lb test) monofilament or black dacron (fly-tying
thread is perfect and very cheap). Tie a tiny loop at one end
and with a six-turn half blood knot tie the other end to the
bend of the hook. In total the hair should be roughly
between ¾ and 1 inch long, no more; although there is
room for experiment here (see fig. 15A). Having sleeved
the bait on to a 'hooked' baiting needle (fig. 15B) catch on
to the loop and gently slide the bait on to the hair. To stop
it from sliding off pop a tiny plastic hair stop into the loop
(fig. 15C) and that's it.

Float ledger rig

To convert the *lift* into a *bolt rig* (or *shock rig*) with or
without the bait on a 'hair', simply pinch on four or five

FIGURE 16 *Convert-*
ing the lift into a bolt/
shock rig

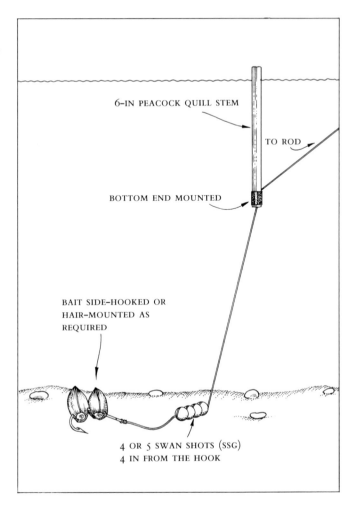

6-IN PEACOCK QUILL STEM

TO ROD

BOTTOM END MOUNTED

BAIT SIDE-HOOKED OR
HAIR-MOUNTED AS
REQUIRED

4 OR 5 SWAN SHOTS (SSG)
4 IN FROM THE HOOK

swan shot instead of the usual two (fig. 16). This invariably stops nuisance fish like bream and tench from pushing the bait about and giving false bites. Be prepared to hold the rod all the time because it is rather tricky fishing, especially with the bait close to lilies or beside jungle swims. When a carp grabs the bait and instantly panics off (hence the name shock or bolt rig), it feels the extra shots as the hook pricks home and it moves at incredible speed.

Converting the standard 'lift' method into a bolt rig is in fact far more practical for tackling weedy or lily-bed swims than ledgering and waiting for a buzzer to sound. Using a float (once you have accepted the fact that the rod must always be held) you can be walking slowly back-

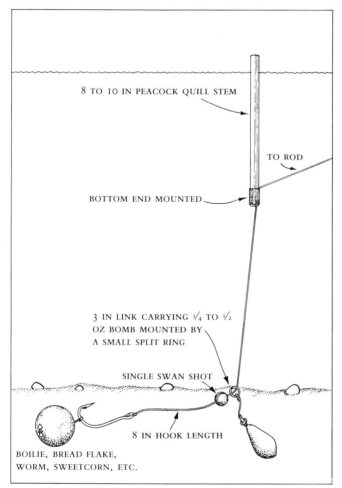

FIGURE 17 *Float ledger rig for distant swims*

8 TO 10 IN PEACOCK QUILL STEM

TO ROD

BOTTOM END MOUNTED

3 IN LINK CARRYING ¼ TO ½ OZ BOMB MOUNTED BY A SMALL SPLIT RING

SINGLE SWAN SHOT

8 IN HOOK LENGTH

BOILIE, BREAD FLAKE, WORM, SWEETCORN, ETC.

wards and bullying a big fish out of tough lily roots at least several seconds quicker than is needed for your brain to react to the noise of a bite alarm and tell your arm to strike, by which time of course the carp has wound 10 yd of line through the lily bed and is probably out through the other side.

To reach distant swims but still enjoy watching a float (not always a practicable technique in windy conditions) thread on a mini running ledger using a ¼ or ½ oz bomb and stop 8 in from the hook with a single swan shot (fig. 17). This simple float ledger rig also works well in deep water swims that are fairly close in to the bank at times when choppy conditions make light float fishing impossible.

Float fishing for crucians

To catch crucians regularly, a very carefully shotted light float rig is imperative, the best floats being a fine tipped antenna or a short, narrow-diameter length of peacock quill fished in 'mini lift' style. The object is to see those tiny bites for which crucians are renowned and which often barely register on the float tip (fig. 18).

For this reason the single shot (a no. 1, BB or AA depending on float size) should be not more than 2 in from the hook. Try moving it even closer, to 1 in away, because sometimes this alone can make all the difference between

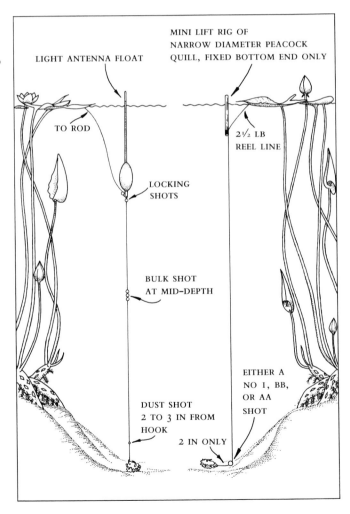

FIGURES 18 AND 19
18 (right) *Mini lift rig for crucians* and 19 (left) *float fishing for crucians*

LIGHT ANTENNA FLOAT

MINI LIFT RIG OF
NARROW DIAMETER PEACOCK
QUILL, FIXED BOTTOM END ONLY

TO ROD

LOCKING SHOTS

2½ LB REEL LINE

BULK SHOT AT MID-DEPTH

DUST SHOT 2 TO 3 IN FROM HOOK

2 IN ONLY

EITHER A NO 1, BB, OR AA SHOT

seeing bites and not. The secret, after casting in and
tightening up so the float cocks, is to wind down even
further so the tip is just the merest 'blimp' on the surface.
And then strike the slightest movement whether it moves
up or down.

When crucians are really feeding confidently (see 'Feeding'), denoted by clusters of small bubbles regularly rising
to the surface, the float might even lift completely out of
the water and lay flat, as the carp tilts its head up after
sucking up the bait and dislodges the shot. Or the tip will
sink positively as the crucian characteristically runs along
the bottom. But far more bites will barely register on the
float, so you need to hold the rod throughout and be eagle-
eyed.

To stand a better chance of hitting bites from crafty
crucians which just lie on the bottom blowing the bait in
and out, rig up a light antenna float with a dust shot 2–3 in
from the hook, the bulk shot set at mid depth (fig. 19).
After carefully plumbing the swim, adjust the float so the
bait is literally a fraction above the bottom. As with the lift
rig, strike at the slightest movement on the float tip.
Remember to keep loose feed or small balls of ground bait
going in on the little-and-often principle, and they might
be encouraged to feed all day. A ruse always worth trying
when they are particularly dour is to gently wind the float
in 6 in at a time, which makes the bait lift upwards
enticingly and gently fall down to the bottom again. Baits
which are inherently buoyant like breadflake or casters, or
which are expected to move such as worms, work best
when 'twitching' in this way to encourage bites.

FLOATER FISHING

Margin fishing

To catch carp slurping down floating baits like crusts or
mixers which have either been scattered amongst the
marginal growth or drifted there with the wind, there
cannot be a more simple rig than using just the hook itself.
If the fish are directly below the rod tip, lower the floater
down so it rests on the surface without any slack line

The best rig for
crucian carp: a single
shot just 2 in from the
hook, and a short
length of peacock quill
attached to the line
with silicone tubing,
fished lift style.

Crucians are always
willing to feed, and
can still be caught
during the heat of a
bright summer's day.
Bites will appear as
the tiniest registration
on the float. To help
combat this and reduce
unwanted glare wear
polaroid glasses and a
sun vizor.

Even modest-sized carp provide long, exciting scraps when hooked close in. Over-hanging tree canopies are the kind of spots beneath which carp feel totally confident in rising to suck in floaters.

lying on the water. Hold the rod loosely yet expectantly with the reel's bale arm closed (the clutch properly set), and in the other hand hold a loop of line pulled from between butt ring and reel (fig. 20). This you let slip through your fingers when a carp closes its mouth over the bait and submerges with it, before whacking the rod back to set the hook.

Many carp anglers would rate this particular form of marginal floater fishing as the most exciting technique of all and I would certainly not give them an argument. It is extremely satisfying, but demands tremendous stealth simply crawling into a position where a bait can be lowered amongst patrolling surface-feeding fish.

When surface activity is slow and the appearance of carp is not expected until the light starts to fade (either due to weather or clear water conditions) quietly set the rod on

LOOP OF LINE LOOSELY HELD

BALE ARM CLOSED

BAIT FLOATS ON THE SURFACE
WITHOUT ANY LINE LYING ON THE WATER   BAIT CAN BE CRUST, MIXER BISCUIT, ETC
TO SCARE THE CARP

FIGURE 20 *Margin fishing (daytime)*

two rests, again with the bale arm closed, and instead of holding the loop of line between butt ring and reel, hang on a lightweight coil indicator. A cylinder of silver foil is perfect (fig. 21).

When fishing this method over marginal lilies, wind the bait so it comes to rest alongside the pads and lay the line over them (fig. 22). Don't for a moment imagine the carp cannot see even small floaters presented in this way. They are looking up into bright light, and can even identify the form of a floater resting completely on top of a lily pad. On numerous occasions I have witnessed carp knocking pads to dislodge a seemingly invisible (to them) unreachable

CLOSED BALE ARM

SILVER FOIL CYLINDER
ON LINE BETWEEN BUTT
RING AND REEL

LINE IS KEPT CLEAR OF WATER
TO PREVENT IT SCARING CARP

FIGURE 21 *Margin fishing (dusk onwards)*

floater. And they are not satisfied until such food is in their stomachs.

When using pieces of floating bread-crust over pads, or drifting them across the surface in open areas, if carp are suspicious of the floating bread use a crust/flake cocktail.

Start by sliding a piece of crust up over the eye of the hook and then squeeze on a giant piece of flake. Slide the crust down again and gently squeeze a part of the flake on to the crust, thus 'locking' them together. Hopefully they will hold together until a carp investigates and 'knocks' them apart, whereupon the flake will slowly start to sink. At this point the carp can stand it no longer and promptly

FIGURE 22 *Fishing over lilies*

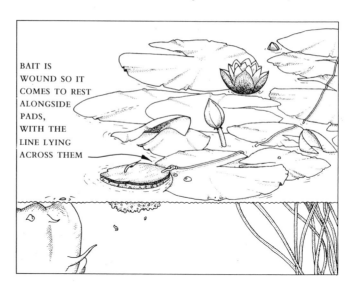

BAIT IS
WOUND SO IT
COMES TO REST
ALONGSIDE
PADS,
WITH THE
LINE LYING
ACROSS THEM

sucks in the flake. Watch the line carefully and hit any positive movement instantly.

Floating controllers

When carp will only accept floaters presented further out because the water along the margins is either too clear, too shallow or both, making them feel vulnerable, casting weight is required in the form of a self-cocking controller (see 'Tackle') like the 'ten-pin', which is available in two sizes, one for distances up to 30 yd, and a larger one for much greater distances. Loose-feed floaters like small biscuits, boilies and so on can all be catapulted into any given area alongside features, and the hook bait deposited accurately among them. Or better still, cast out the controller and hook bait well up wind; then catapult the loose feed around it, allowing the floating food to drift down wind whilst playing out line from an open (well-filled) spool.

Rig up a 'ten-pin' by threading the reel line (which should be liberally greased with mucilin so it floats well) through the swivel. Then thread on a small bead and tie on the hook. Anywhere from 2 to 6 ft above the hook, tie on a sliding stop knot against which the bead and finally the controller will come to rest (fig. 23A). Alternatively, after threading on the tenpin and bead, tie on a small swivel and

This young fisherman looks deservedly happy with a superbly conditioned common carp. It was taken on a small cube of bread crust presented with a 'ten-pin' loaded controller.

FIGURE 23 *Floating controllers*

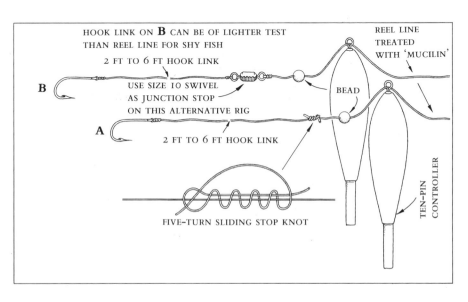

HOOK LINK ON **B** CAN BE OF LIGHTER TEST THAN REEL LINE FOR SHY FISH

2 FT TO 6 FT HOOK LINK

REEL LINE TREATED WITH 'MUCILIN'

B

USE SIZE 10 SWIVEL AS JUNCTION STOP ON THIS ALTERNATIVE RIG

BEAD

A

2 FT TO 6 FT HOOK LINK

FIVE–TURN SLIDING STOP KNOT

TEN–PIN CONTROLLER

to its other end add the hook link. This may be lighter than the reel line (if carp are really spooky), and anywhere from 2 to 6 ft long – even 10 ft long if you can cast it. Start with a 4 ft long hook link, however, for easy casting and finish the rig by adding the hook (fig. 23 B). For large baits use hook sizes 6 to 8, while small floaters are more naturally presented on a strong, forged, size 10 or even size 12 provided conditions allow.

Tactics

Carp are invariably more wary of accepting surface baits once they have associated them with danger than they are of bottom-fished baits. But by fishing as light as you dare, using much finer line than normal, for instance 6 lb test instead of 10 lb test if conditions permit, and by fishing during periods of low light at dusk, dawn or even well on into darkness, most problems can be solved. Carp refuse the bait because they can see the line and hook, or because the bait behaves unlike all the free offerings around it due to the weight of the hook and drag from the line. Carp prove this time and time again by mopping up all the free floaters, but not the one on the hook. It is frustration personified. The problem is not so much getting them to accept floating food but to accept the hook bait. Even familiar unattached baits like pieces of bread crust are taken down, maybe not so quickly on waters regularly fished, but disappear they eventually will. Particle baits create far less suspicion, and sooner or later one will be sucked in, provided carp respond.

In contrast to bottom baits, at least it's possible to actually observe the reaction of carp and consequently do something about the way in which the bait is refused. Anything and everything is worth trying. Go for a much longer hook link to create less drag; or smaller hook; two floaters instead of one, which provides greater buoyancy; grease or even degrease the hook link, and so on.

If all else fails, put your faith in the hair rig (fig. 24) and offer the bait off the hook. Rig the floater up sleeved on to a fine mono or dacron 1 in hair, and support the hook so it floats horizontally on the surface by threading a length of 3 mm duplon (rod-handle material) on to the shank. There

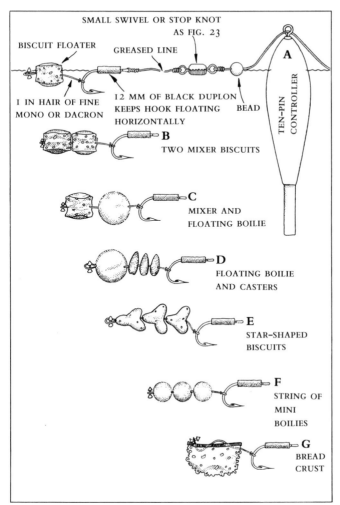

FIGURE 24 *Hair-rig floaters*

are all sorts of variations worth trying along these lines. Go down in hook size: try two or even three floaters on the hair instead of one; or a cocktail, one biscuit and one boilie together on the same hair, a boilie and casters, and so on.

Offering a floating bait is perhaps the most selective of all big carp methods, because you can actually watch the fish of your dreams close its great lips over the bait. You can even pull the bait away from lesser fish should the commotion of hooking one scare off a monster which is one amongst a group of modest-sized carp.

Because the line actually passes through the top of the controller, when a carp moves away with the bait the line

There is nothing too deliberate or choosy about the way in which these two mirror carp are munching through a batch of dog-biscuit floaters. When they eventually wise up to floaters presented straight on the hook, offer the bait on a fine hair rig.

will visibly tighten and 'lift' across the surface. Hold the rod all the time with the bale arm closed ready for action. Straighten any bow in the line formed by wind drift, leaving just a little slack so as not to scare interested fish through resistance. Keep your eyes fixed on the float's red top and identify your hook bait amongst the loose ones, striking on sight if you suddenly see it go without the line actually moving or whistling through the float.

Not all carp belt off. Some merely sink slowly beneath the surface and munch merrily away. Remember the controller float is not designed to go under, simply to take the bait out anywhere from 10 to 50 yd. At distances beyond this, casting and wind drift problems hamper float control and striking.

Fishing at distance

The answer to distance problems is the *anchored floater* presented on a sliding, buoyant paternoster rig (fig. 25). Retain the 4 ft hook link and swap the float for a long paternoster link consisting of a 1½ oz bomb at the bottom and a swivel at the top, with a buoyant sub-float body which slides freely in between. A buoyant bead up against

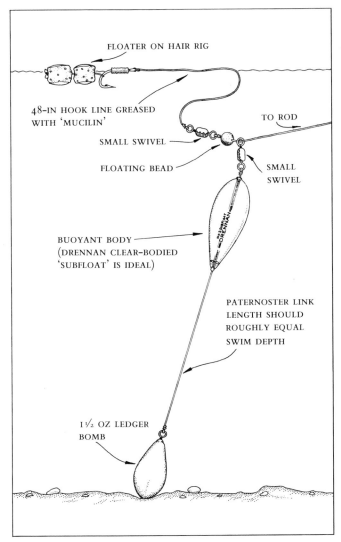

FLOATER ON HAIR RIG

48-IN HOOK LINE GREASED
WITH 'MUCILIN'

TO ROD

SMALL SWIVEL

FLOATING BEAD

SMALL
SWIVEL

BUOYANT BODY
(DRENNAN CLEAR-BODIED
'SUBFLOAT' IS IDEAL)

PATERNOSTER LINK
LENGTH SHOULD
ROUGHLY EQUAL
SWIM DEPTH

1½ OZ LEDGER
BOMB

FIGURE 25 *Anchored
floater for distance
fishing*

the small junction swivel helps flotation. This link should
measure approximately the depth of the swim. When the
rig lands and the bomb touches bottom, the buoyant float
body rises up to the swivel and supports the reel line just a
couple of feet below the surface with the bait floating
nicely above.

Tighten up gently with the rod set horizontal in two
rests, ensuring the line is sunk, and clip on an indicator,
such as bobbin or monkey climber. Keep the bale arm
closed. When a carp sucks in the floater, the reel line runs
freely through the paternoster swivel, up goes the indicator

and you are in business with a hefty strike to pick up any loose line.

For this kind of long-range floater fishing, keep your eyes peeled on the area of the hook bait with binoculars so you can anticipate a probable run if you sight carp in the vicinity, and use wind direction plus your catapult to scatter loose floaters around the anchored hook bait.

LEDGERING

A basic multi-purpose rig

FIGURE 26 *A basic multi-purpose rig (the running link ledger)*

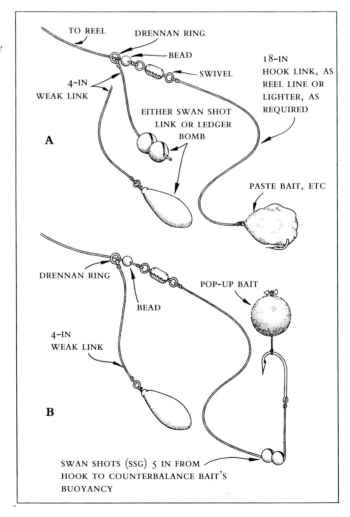

TO REEL   DRENNAN RING

BEAD

SWIVEL

4-IN
WEAK LINK

18-IN
HOOK LINK, AS
REEL LINE OR
LIGHTER, AS
REQUIRED

EITHER SWAN SHOT
LINK OR LEDGER
BOMB

A

PASTE BAIT, ETC

DRENNAN RING

BEAD

POP-UP BAIT

4-IN
WEAK LINK

B

SWAN SHOTS (SSG) 5 IN FROM
HOOK TO COUNTERBALANCE BAIT'S
BUOYANCY

For ledgering pieces of soft paste, cubes of meat, perhaps a couple of cockles, in diminutive waters where belt-off runs are neither expected nor desired, use a simple running link ledger as in fig. 26A.

Where a carp could go ploughing through weeds or snags, the ledger link, to which is attached a small bomb or swan shots, should be of a considerably lighter test than the reel line. Thus it creates a weak link which will break off when caught up in weeds, leaving the carp still connected to the main line.

FIGURE 27 *A heavier multi-purpose rig*

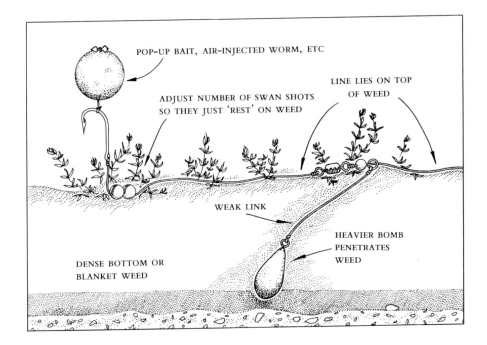

POP-UP BAIT, AIR-INJECTED WORM, ETC

LINE LIES ON TOP OF WEED

ADJUST NUMBER OF SWAN SHOTS SO THEY JUST 'REST' ON WEED

WEAK LINK

HEAVIER BOMB PENETRATES WEED

DENSE BOTTOM OR BLANKET WEED

For presenting pop-up baits, such as an air-injected lobworm or any of the floating baits (usually fished on the surface), fix on one or two swan shots 5 in from the hook to counterbalance the bait's buoyancy as in fig. 26B.

When fishing over dense bottom or blanket weed simply extend the ledger link to compensate, and use a heavier bomb for penetration down to the bottom (fig. 27). Experiment in the margins where you can see the rig working until you are happy.

Scorching runs are sometimes experienced with this set-up should the rig become hung up in weed. Generally, however, the indicator (monkey climber or coil) rises

positively upwards, usually with enough time for an unhurried strike. Coupled to a buzzer the warning is quite adequate when sitting beside the rod. As I play fish from a pre-adjusted clutch, the anti-reverse is always on, enabling me at any point to grab the rod one-handed if necessary without the handle whizzing round.

Opposite: Admiring the carp before carefully returning it is all part of the enjoyment.

The bolt rig

Now we arrive at what in recent years has become the panacea to catching carp: the *bolt* or *shock rig* ledger. Sadly, people use no other technique because it is so effective. I have left the bolt rig until last because I wish you, the reader, to treat its use as such: a 'deadly' method for catching 'difficult carp' – carp which are so wary they won't provide enough indications on other methods of presentation for you to strike and hook them. These other methods of varying skill and technique, most of which have already been covered, open up the entire exciting carp fishing world and enable you to value and catch carp of all shapes and sizes from a diverse variety of fisheries. The bolt rig also allows you this enjoyment, and at the end of the day you choose that which provides the most pleasure.

It's a fact that carp do not fall for the same tackle rig time after time. Bites which started out as slammers on simple ledger tackle soon become 'twitches', so imperceptible they are impossible to strike. And this is when the 'bolt rig' comes into its own. Using a heavy lead ($1\frac{1}{2}$ to 2 oz) which is felt by the carp just as it sucks the bait from the bottom back to its throat teeth for chewing, shocks that carp into closing its lips and doing a runner. In short it 'bolts off'. In the process it forgets about the bait and the hook is pulled home. The secret is in having exactly the right distance from lead to bait, which obviously varies with different-sized carp.

A distance somewhere between 6 to 10 in from hook to lead is favoured. The bait (boilies and hard particles such as beans or peanuts, etc., work best with this method) can simply be side-hooked (fig. 28A) or slid on to a 'hair' (fig. 28B), providing the carp with extra confidence when it sucks it in. In each case the hook link can be of monofilament (reel line), black or multi-coloured dacron

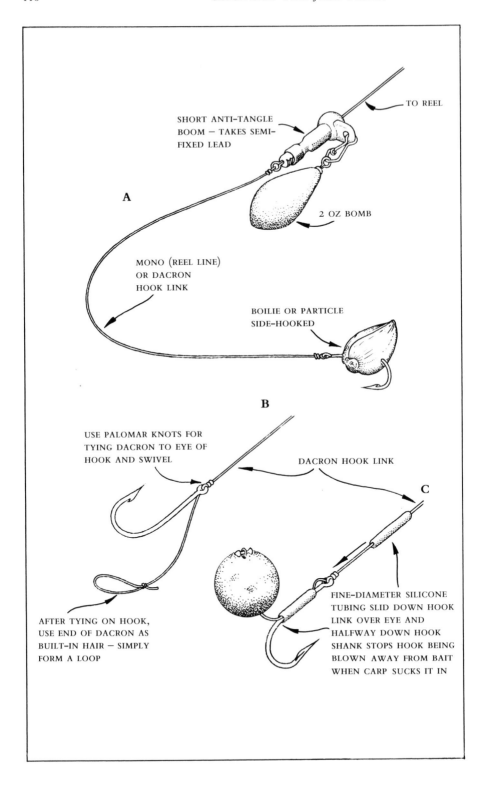

SHORT ANTI-TANGLE
BOOM – TAKES SEMI-
FIXED LEAD

TO REEL

A

2 OZ BOMB

MONO (REEL LINE)
OR DACRON
HOOK LINK

BOILIE OR PARTICLE
SIDE-HOOKED

B

USE PALOMAR KNOTS FOR
TYING DACRON TO EYE OF
HOOK AND SWIVEL

DACRON HOOK LINK

C

AFTER TYING ON HOOK,
USE END OF DACRON AS
BUILT-IN HAIR – SIMPLY
FORM A LOOP

FINE–DIAMETER SILICONE
TUBING SLID DOWN HOOK
LINK OVER EYE AND
HALFWAY DOWN HOOK
SHANK STOPS HOOK BEING
BLOWN AWAY FROM BAIT
WHEN CARP SUCKS IT IN

or braid, or of floss which separates into numerous gossamer strands and becomes virtually invisible on the bottom (see 'Hook lengths', p. 52).

FIGURE 28 (Opposite) *The bolt or shock rig*

With dacron hook lengths, after tying the hook on don't clip the end off short. Simply tie in a small loop and use it as a 'built in' hair.

To stop the hook being blown away from the bait when a carp sucks it in, sleeve a short length of fine-diameter clear or black silicone tubing down the hook link over the eye and onto the shank, thus shortening the hair length (fig. 28C).

Note from fig. 28A that the (semi-fixed) 2 oz lead is attached to the clip of a short boom which threads on to the reel line above the hook link swivel and stops the lead from tangling. There are numerous types of anti-tangle ledger rig bits now available, almost as much choice, in fact, as the match fisherman has in floats. Much of it is superfluous, and only helps to deter carp from approaching the bait. So my advice is to keep your terminal rig as simple as possible. With this in mind consider my 'simple bolt fig' in fig. 29. The short hook link and reel line are

FIGURE 29 *A simple bolt rig*

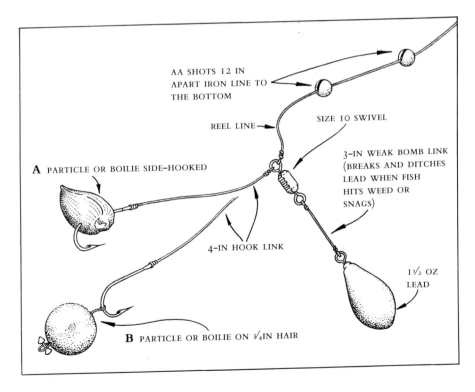

AA SHOTS 12 IN APART IRON LINE TO THE BOTTOM

REEL LINE →

SIZE 10 SWIVEL

A PARTICLE OR BOILIE SIDE-HOOKED

3-IN WEAK BOMB LINK (BREAKS AND DITCHES LEAD WHEN FISH HITS WEED OR SNAGS)

4-IN HOOK LINK

1½ OZ LEAD

B PARTICLE OR BOILIE ON ¾IN HAIR

What every carp angler loves to see, fish rising freely to surface baits in a quiet corner of a beautiful lake.

both connected to the same end of a tiny-size 10 swivel, so that should it break in half you are still playing the carp, while the 'weak' bomb link is tied to the other end of the swivel. Lengths of both hook and bomb links can be varied to suit bottom or weed of varying types, but overall a hook link of 4 in and a bomb link of 3 in are ideal.

The beauty of this rig is its 'simplicity', and the fact that should a carp go belting off through heavy weed the weak link soon ditches the lead. It is also excellent for presenting pop-up baits on the hair rig above dense bottom weed (see fig. 30). If the bottom weed is deeper than the 3 in lead link, simply alter it accordingly. Note the three AA shots pinched at 12 in intervals up the line from the swivels, which iron the reel line to the weed or hide it in soft silt so as not to scare carp as they approach the bait. To hide the reel line, dip the rod tip beneath the surface after casting, and with the left hand (assuming you are holding the rod in your right hand) gently pull the line until it is straight. Then allow a little slack from the reel and lift the rod horizontally on to the rests.

Opposite: *The bolt rig/boilie combination presented 50 yd out on a shallow bar accounted for this fine Norfolk specimen.*

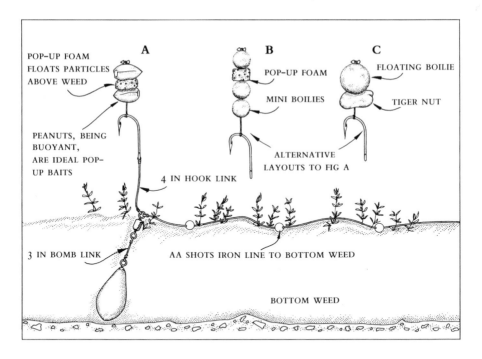

POP-UP FOAM
FLOATS PARTICLES
ABOVE WEED

A

B

POP-UP FOAM

C

FLOATING BOILIE

MINI BOILIES

TIGER NUT

PEANUTS, BEING
BUOYANT,
ARE IDEAL POP-
UP BAITS

ALTERNATIVE
LAYOUTS TO FIG A

4 IN HOOK LINK

3 IN BOMB LINK

AA SHOTS IRON LINE TO BOTTOM WEED

BOTTOM WEED

FIGURE 30 *Pop-up bolt rig*

Contrary to popular belief, the line from bolt rig to rod does not necessarily need to be 'hauser' tight in order for the hook point to be driven home. The lead in conjunction with the speed at which a carp panics off are responsible for this. So wherever possible leave a slight bow in the line from rod tip to surface. This means the line close to the bolt rig will be lying along the bottom contours and not inhibiting carp in crystal-clear water from approaching the bait.

There is perhaps a better hooking rate once the carp has picked up the bait presented on a 'tight line' from lead to rod. But if a proportion of runs do not happen because the carp sensed the 'bowstring line' and departed, it does not help you catch more fish.

Whenever there is a strong undertow in large waters, as in windy conditions, it is of course impossible to fish a gentle bow. Then it has to be a tight line 'clipped up' or nothing. At the reel end, after putting the line beneath the 'monkey', open the bale arm and neatly catch the line beneath a run clip fixed around the handle directly opposite the spool (see fig. 31). When a carp grabs the bait and promptly does a runner, line spews from the open spool while the monkey body drops a couple of inches, held

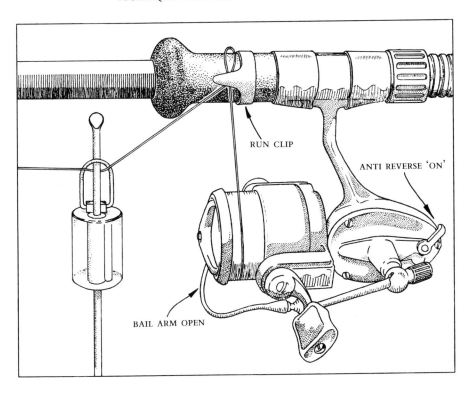

RUN CLIP

ANTI REVERSE 'ON'

BAIL ARM OPEN

there through the sheer speed of line evaporating from the open spool, while the buzzer screams its head off.

Figure 31 *Clipping up the line*

If using a reel with a bait runner facility, the bale arm will of course already be closed while the spool itself revolves. For both situations, a hefty strike is not required; indeed it could even prove disastrous. Simply close the bale arm by winding forward (which also puts the bait runner reel back into gear with a pre-set clutch) and gently bend the rod back into the fish when all is nicely tight. It is a very stereotyped and easy method to master.

In confined overgrown fisheries where the erection of rod rest set-ups, buzzers and monkey climbers could ruin the chances of carp even patrolling close by, let alone picking up a bolt-rigged bait-up, I fish in a very basic, effective, if rather risky way. As I never leave the rod or rods (I occasionally use two rods, though for much of my carp fishing, because it is based on opportunity rather than patience, I use just one) after placing the bait accurately and ensuring the line is nicely sunk along the bottom (hence my preference for two or three AA shots spread along the line above the lead), I simply lay the rod down on the

*Whether you prefer
fishing with the bait
anchored to the bottom
with a 3 oz lead, or
feeling for bites in the
dark with the line
hooked around your
index finger, there is
no more exciting sight
than observing carp
confidently mopping
up floaters from the
surface.*

carpet of marginal plants. I use no rod rests or alarms, but the anti-reverse is on and the clutch is set a shade lighter than I intend playing a fish with.

One minute there is nothing. The very next there is a furrow on the surface (if fishing shallow water) as a carp panics off, easily setting the hook and jerking the rod across the marginal plants in the process. I said it was a risky technique and indeed it is. But honestly, after taking goodness knows how many double-figure carp by this method from numerous fisheries, certainly well over 100, I have yet to be broken or to lose the rod. But it's not for the faint-hearted.

Good carping

INDEX

Catch
TENCH

CONTENTS

ACKNOWLEDGEMENTS

No angling writer can produce a book without considerable help from others. Allow me therefore to thank the editing and design team, the mates who leave their own fishing to photograph me, and a very special thank you to good friend Dave Batten who has made such a fine job of the line drawings.

John Wilson
Great Witchingham
1991

INTRODUCTION

A S I sincerely trust the reader will discover within the following pages, there is a surfeit of interesting, challenging and exciting methods of catching tench. Space has prevented me from providing details of every conceivable technique: indeed, would it not be rather presumptuous even to suggest that I know them all. For I am sure I do not. That is the everlasting strength and wonder of our sport. No one ever knows it all and we never stop learning from each other, from the environment in which we live and fish, and of course from the fish themselves.

This book is therefore a collection of my experiences and thoughts on tench fishing covering a wide spectrum of still waters and rivers, paying great detail in so far as location is concerned to the kinds of habitat in which tench prefer to live. After all, I know of no better way of contacting another person than by knocking on their front door. And to be successful at catching tench, whatever its size, this invariably proves the most rewarding approach.

I have purposefully avoided the trap of advising you on how best to catch specimen tench because this is a book of techniques which, once practised, open the door to catching tench of all sizes, wherever you fish.

Besides, exactly at what size does a tench become a specimen? Is it the traditional yardstick of 5 lb (which I still hold sacred), or fish of 7, 8 and 9 lb which nowadays are being regularly taken from selected southern fisheries, particularly rich reservoirs and mature gravel pits.

I rather imagine the angler with limited local prospects of overstocked ponds and small pits where tench average between 2 and 3 lb would be overjoyed at capturing a 4-pounder. And the northerner with only the local canal to fish would indeed be happy with a tench of half that weight.

So please learn to appreciate the species as a creature and each technique as just one route among many towards its capture. Techniques you can vary, adjust and enjoy experimenting with throughout an entire lifetime – come on, come and catch some tench with me.

CHAPTER ONE

THE
SPECIES

TENCH
(*Tinca tinca*)

With its distinctive olive green livery, tiny red 'teddy bear eyes' and dark grey-brown fins, the tench is seldom confused, by fishermen, with any other species. Even those who never practise the gentle art will know of the tench by its odd name and be aware of its green body, for there is not another freshwater species so unusually coloured. Yet we take its unique friendly form for granted.

Even with the escalating popularity of carp during the past few years, the tench remains a firm summer favourite amongst UK anglers and their counterparts in most European countries, although European anglers unfortunately are not so keen on returning tench of an edible size. Its delicate, sweet, white flesh is highly prized right across the continent, and in Asia where tench are intensively farmed for food.

A phenomenon surrounding the tench and no other species, something which has been handed down over the years from one angling writer to another, is its nickname of 'doctor fish'. It used to be thought that a tench only needs to rub up against a fish of another species ailing from open wounds, and it's on the mend. Well, maybe its thick coating of slime does contain some kind of medicinal property, no one really seems to know for sure. I certainly cannot remember, having caught thousands of tench over the years, catching one with wounds which have not healed over.

In a particular, very shallow estate lake that I fish in north Norfolk for instance, where the owner's son regularly water skis throughout the summer, it is nothing out of the ordinary to catch tench with horrendous wounds across their bodies. Some of these may well be the

With their incredibly thick coating of body mucus, which homogenizes broken tissue quickly, tench are able to survive horrendous injuries, whether caused by a pike attack, or, as in this case, the propellor of an outboard motor.

results of attack by large pike, which the lake is known to contain, but a percentage I am sure are propeller wounds from a powerful outboard engine. Yet in all cases these lacerations are perfectly healed and homogenized in that thick layer of body mucus for which the tench is renowned. Species such as roach or bream have scales that are dislodged easily through bad handling or from predator attack, with the possibility of secondary infection setting in and maybe even premature death. The tench, however, has the tiniest of flat scales, deeply embedded in a tough skin and coated in protective slime of the most tenacious rubberized texture.

Everything about the tench suggests strength and durability – its thick-set, oval body shape, incredibly large, rounded fins and particularly thick tail root. Small wonder they fight so doggedly. The males appear noticeably chunky and shorter than the females, and are easily distinguishable by their 'crinkly' spoon-shaped pelvic fins, the second ray of which is enlarged, and by the lumpy muscles or 'gonads' just above the pelvic fin. When gently compressed against the body the pelvics completely hide the male's vent, whereas the neater, almost pointed pelvic fins of the female do not. The mouth, which if anything is upward pointing (one reason why tench must stand on

It is easier to distinguish between the sexes with tench than any other species. Look at the crinkly pelvic fins that cover the vent and almost touch the anal fin in the male on the left, with lumpy protruding muscles or gonads immediately above. Then compare with the smooth, classic lines of the female on the right.

their heads when feeding from the bottom – see 'Feeding') with thick-rimmed rubber lips, has a tiny barbel at each corner and is semi-protrusible.

Situated in the back of its throat are the powerful pharyngeal teeth used for mincing larger food items into pulp for swallowing. Maggots, for instance, which reappear as mere skins have obviously been crushed by the pharyngeal teeth, the soft insides sucked out and the unwanted parts (including your hook) spat out, even though the bite was not identified at the time. Because these teeth are never seen (unless you cut them from a decaying fish) most anglers would perhaps not realize tench are so equipped. But like all cyprinids (even gudgeon and dace have them), tench could not masticate their food without these flatish plates of bone, which are not dissimilar to those of the crucian carp.

Tench are a decidedly lethargic, ponderous fish. They

thrive best in stillwaters, slow-moving stretches of lowland rivers, canals, drains and so on, especially where vegetation is dense, because from soft weeds it obtains much of its natural diet – insect larvae, snails, shrimps, anellus, water boatmen, and so on. It also gorges on free-roaming zooplanktons such as daphnia, the largest of the water fleas, and is well equipped to siphon through the detritus, that first few inches of decaying bottom vegetation, in search of annelid worms and midge larvae (see 'Feeding'). It never seems to be bothered by the lack of oxygen down amongst the silt, and is probably more tolerant of low levels of dissolved oxygen than any other freshwater species.

A curiosity regarding the tench, and a question I am often asked, is how long do they live. Similar to other cyprinids, such as carp and bream, tench are known to grow (in length that is) for anything up to 12–15 years. Once they have stopped growing, and a length of 25–26 in seems to be around the optimum length for the species (although most average between 18–22 in), there is nothing to say that like carp tench do not carry on living for a further 15–20 years, maybe even longer. So a realistic life span of 25–30 years should therefore not be discounted.

I am of the opinion that many of the tench inhabiting certain broads and shallow estate lakes that I have fished regularly throughout the last 20 years are the very same tench I encountered when I first fished there. Their average size of between 4 lb and 6 lb fluctuates a little each year due to the availability of natural food at the time, and of course if they spawn particularly late the females weigh considerably more than they did the previous year at around the same time. And these seasonal weight fluctuations are probably the reason why we tend not to consider that they are indeed the same lovely old tench being caught year after year, just as we have learnt to recognize carp as individuals. They even look old, some are decidedly battle-scarred, with marks and nodules on their lips from being repeatedly caught over the years and healed lacerations from past encounters with herons and pike.

Whilst talking about tench being taken by pike, I have over the years experienced numerous attacks even when playing large fish. I remember one particular occasion in the early 1970s when tench fishing Beeston Lake near

Wroxham (which at one time held the British bream record for a monster of 13 lb 9 oz caught by Mike Davison) when right out of the blue a huge pike grabbed the tench I was playing and it was no small one at that – it looked to be all of 6 lb plus (at that time it would probably have been the largest I had ever caught from Beeston). As it swirled on the surface in 3 ft of water just beyond the rod tip, almost ready for netting, from the corner of one eye I suddenly noticed a huge furrow appear in the weedy margins to my right. The furrow headed straight for the tench, there was an almighty boil on the surface where-upon the line suddenly went limp and then all went calm. I stood there absolutely dumb-founded, and I am sure several seconds elapsed before my brain registered the obvious. I just couldn't believe that such a large specimen as a 6 lb plus tench could be grabbed by a pike, but it had been and I was furious.

There is, however, a happy ending to the story. I was so incensed at the pike that I caught some small rudd to wobble as deadbaits and tried to catch it, actually landing three double-figure pike within as many minutes. Each was particularly thin, almost on the starvation line and weighed a good third less than they should have. Two weighed around 12 lb a piece and the biggest a shade under 19 lb. At 44 in long I should perhaps have been looking at a near 30-pounder, for its head was simply enormous. Obviously the big tench had managed (as most do) to slip away from its grip, unless I caught the wrong pike, which is doubtful because I took a few more emaciated fish and moved the whole lot to nearby Barton Broad where they would be most appreciated and hopefully regain their weight loss. And the 44 in-long tench-grabber was by far the largest.

As a point of interest, the reason that the entire pike stock decided to diet simultaneously was one of simple lack of food. The club who controlled the fishing at Beeston, which the previous year was so full of roach and rudd up to the pound, found that their members were not getting their baits through to the tench, and decided to even the odds by having some of the shoal fish removed. The trouble was that being a small, shallow lake it was easy to net and unbeknown to the club the netman must have removed 99 per cent of the fodder fish, resulting a

The capture of massive tench of 7 and even 8 lb is now considered an everyday event from certain southern reservoirs and gravel pits. However, catches like this quintet of lift-caught beauties weighing between 3½ and 5½ lb are what tench fishing is all about.

few months later in the starving pike attacking anything which moved.

Another curiosity that has occurred only during the last decade or so is the fact that in a fair proportion of fisheries tench are now attaining very much larger weights than ever before – the current British record being a monster of 14 lb 3 oz caught by Phil Gooriah from Wrasbury pits in 1987. For instance, for over 30 years up until 1963 the tench record had slowly increased from 7 lb to just over 9 lb. Yet as I write this, tench of 7 lb and 8 lb are everyday catches in certain southern fisheries, particularly the rich gravel pits in Kent, Hertfordshire and Oxfordshire.

For a high-value specimen these days enthusiasts in the know are looking towards tench of 9 lb plus, a fish which, as I have said, 30 years ago would have broken the record.

Lots of theories have been put forward as to why this is happening, of course. The favourite is that the huge quantities of high-nutritional-value paste and boiled baits that have been introduced (initially to attract carp), and which the tench have subsequently learnt to accept as natural food, has resulted in their growing very much larger. Certainly, the number of tench taken nowadays

over 9 lb and 10 lb is completely mind-boggling; it is rather strange to anglers who have been around long enough to monitor the scene for the last 30 or 40 years, because it has all happened so comparatively recently and with only tench, no other species.

However, is it really all down to the high-nutritional-value (HNV) baits? I have my doubts about this. Certainly the fluctuating seasons and weather patterns we are now

Females that are still carrying spawn during the early season should be handled with extreme care. They could possibly weigh as much as 2– 3 lb more than their natural body weight.

With distinct black eyes and irregular black flecks over a bright yellow body, the rare golden tench is nicknamed 'banana fish'. Strangely, it does not appear to hybridize with the common green tench, and exists in only a handful of fisheries within the British Isles.

experiencing on a global scale surely have some bearing on the matter, although it's difficult to isolate a direct link other than because the summers on average start later, more tench are caught at the beginning of the season so grossly over-full with spawn they weigh considerably heavier than their natural weight, probably by 2–3 lb.

To counter-balance this view, completely spawned-out tench of 8 lb and 9 lb are regularly taken every year nowadays from some of the Kent gravel pits. So where are we? What is even more interesting and in complete contrast to gravel pit fisheries, where the tench may well have reached far greater weight partly through feeding regularly on HNV baits, is the fact that reservoirs like the Tring group in Hertfordshire, which are rich only in zoo planktons and other completely natural foods, are now producing more tench in excess of that magical 10 lb barrier than any other fisheries. And these are waters which have *not* been mass baited over a period of years with HNV carp baits. So exactly why tench are now averaging much larger weights in a selection of fisheries spread over southern England I shall leave you to puzzle out. At least the phenomenon pinpoints waters where these jumbo fish are to be found. Not that any of this makes the slightest bit of real difference to the enjoyment of catching tench as a species, because even 2- and 3-pounders will, on the right tackle, put up an exciting fight. Fish of between 4 and 5 lb are the backbone of quality tench fishing and should always be regarded as such. And personally I still rate tench of 5 lb plus as the realistic goal to aim for. Remember we are talking here in terms of general tench fishing.

GOLDEN TENCH

This beautiful, quite breathtaking creature is more an aquariast's fish than an angler's quarry, though it does exist in a handful of fisheries around the country, particularly those without large predators like pike, which is not difficult to understand. To a predator the golden tench right from the fry stage must stand out like the proverbial sore thumb, just like albino fish, so their survival rate with every creature trying to get in on the act, including the ever-watchful heron, must be miniscule.

Often nicknamed 'banana fish', the golden tench is indeed the colour of a ripe banana even down to the black spots irregularly flecked over its body, though I have seen a fair number of golden tench completely free of any dark markings. It also sports a black eye, pink, translucent, rather petite fins, and overall a much slimmer profile than the common green tench. It is thus by comparison a poor fighter, nowhere near so powerful, though dogged nonetheless. Optimum size rarely exceeds 3 lb and this is large for the golden tench.

As with green tench the males are distinguishable from the females by their spoon-shaped pelvic fins and the lumpy muscles or gonads immediately above them.

Strangely the two types, green and golden, to the best of my knowledge do not inter-breed or throw up mutants. Occasionally one catches a green tench etched with purple markings or blotches all over its head and body. But these I have always taken to be colour disorders in the pigmentation rather like purplish birth marks. Such markings have nothing to do with inter-breeding between golden and green tench.

CHAPTER TWO

ABOUT TENCH

FEEDING

Compared to carp for example, especially when living alongside and therefore in direct competition with them, tench come a poor second in making full use of the natural food at their disposal. They are by nature nowhere near so aggressive, and in reality are probably the most deliberate feeders of all freshwater fish. For tench to grow large they require an exceptionally rich environment, and only in such circumstances are both tench and carp able to attain huge proportions living together. Even then tench still need to outnumber the carp. Switched the other way around, carp will eat them out of house and home.

On really heavily stocked carp fisheries with next to no weed from which the tench can eek a living, and where the water is kept in a continual state of turbidity from the sheer number of carp feeding from the bottom at various times of the day, tench may not even be able to exist beyond a weight of 1 lb or so. Miniature tench of a few ounces seem able to grow amongst densely stocked carp because their infant food requirements are different. But once they require larger food particles higher up the chain, carp rule the roost and the tench can never reach anywhere near their full growth potential. Even adult tench of fully 2 to 3 lb purchased from fish farmers by clubs and lake-owners for stocking into densely populated carp fisheries can never compete. Inevitably they become thinner and thinner, barely scratching a living and merely surviving at half their normal body weight (and it is surprising just how thin tench can become) before being reduced to starvation by the carp. Obviously, these are uncommon circumstances but events I have witnessed on a handful of club waters where the members have thought a second species was needed without realizing the consequences.

As tench kindly pin-point their position when feeding heavily at dawn by sending up patches of tiny bubbles, the best way of locating them is to scan the surface with binoculars.

Having located tench bubbling close into the marginal weeds of this large gravel pit, wheelchair angler Robbie Robertson finds the successful method is to pole-fish a single caster just above the bottom weed beneath a waggler.

In the two small carp lakes that I control, for instance, both densely populated with carp and catfish up to 20 lb, the tench grow thick and chunky-looking up to about 12 oz and are perfectly healthy, but never get any bigger. I suppose the tench is just too slow and ponderous for its own good.

The nice thing about tench when they are feeding in earnest is that they often (though not always) send bubbles up to the surface to tell you where they are. If you watch the surface very carefully (never forget the binoculars – even for close-range observation they are indispensible) the route of each individual fish can usually be followed simply by relating to the groups of bubbles as they appear. In heavily pre-baited swims full of numbers of fish all moving agitatedly about, when the surface looks to all intents and purposes like a witches' cauldron, this just isn't possible. But in swims occupied by just a handful of tench, following the bubbles of individuals can prove almost as fascinating as hooking into one of them. Wherever strong-limbed trees overhang the swim, endeavour to reach a position overhead where you can look directly into the area (providing the water is clear) and observe the stream of bubbles rising from the tench. It teaches you so much about the fish's behaviour. There are in fact various kinds of bubbles attributed to tench which rise to the surface and you must learn to identify them. The tiny 'needle' bubbles made by the tench itself, which escape through its gill filaments as a result of it masticating its food, are perhaps the easiest to identify. Large patches of frothy bubbles, on the other hand, gases released from rotten vegetation in silty waters by the tench in their search for blood-worms, (midge larvae) their favourite natural food, just might be the work of carp or eels. So beware, even experienced anglers come to grief with these gas bubbles on occasion, and view anything 'frothy' with an open mind.

Tench also send up small groups of bubbles in clusters of just two or three, five or six at a time when they are feeding over hard gravel. These are noticeably smaller than those produced by carp, and so there should be little confusion. They are made when the tench stands on its head to suck up baits one at a time and rights itself to chew them, thus emitting only a limited amount. It then moves on a foot or so to the next food item (a grain of corn, piece of flake, etc) and another small group of bubbles rise upwards.

The interpretation and identification of bubbles, and matching them to particular fish, is almost a separate hobby. So try whenever you are given the opportunity to observe tench feeding in crystal-clear water. As an experiment, take a landing-net pole or a bank stick and watch what happens on the surface when you rupture the detritus, that decaying top layer of bottom silt, just as a tench might do when it characteristically stands on its head and with a thrust of its tail runs its nose along the bottom to dislodge and throw up particles of natural food. This of course is why raking or dragging a silty swim proves so effective (pp. 81–84) the tench has its work done for it.

Tench are unquestionably at their most difficult to tempt when they are preoccupied on microscopic food items, in particular zooplankton such as daphnia. There is no mistaking this transparent water flea whose body is tinged a red-brown colour. When it is blown into the margins by wind drift or a strong underwater tow, the concentrations are so thick it's impossible to see the bottom even through gin-clear water. It appears to all intents and purposes as though the water is littered with brick dust. And during the warmer months when daphnia multiplies rapidly, it is to tench what krill is to whales.

I have witnessed numbers of tench lying idly on the bottom of warm, clear, shallow water along margins that are stacked with huge daphnia concentrations, simply gorging themselves completely oblivious to any other food item. I have, believe it or not, lowered a single maggot on an 18 hook tied direct to 2 lb line on to their noses and watched in sheer amazement as it tumbled over the lips and down to the bottom, cast after cast, without the slightest interest being shown. It was as if the maggot did not exist. A bunch of brandlings was given similar treatment, although eventually I did on one occasion 'tweak' at what must have been the right moment, for the tench promptly sucked them in.

Then again, as they were lying there drinking in a gullet-full of daphnia with every breath, perhaps the worms simply went in with the fleas. The area was shared with several large eels also gorging on daphnia, and each similarly positioned, tails stabilized in the silt and their

bodies held in suspension off the bottom like serpents. I would never have believed that eels could by nature refuse a bunch of fresh worms, but these did. As with the tench, even when the worms were lowered on to the eels' gaping mouths, it was as though they were invisible. Such was the draw of and preoccupation with daphnia.

So frustrated was I by this chain of events that on the following morning I went armed with a small mesh aquarium net, a packet of aspic and a flask of hot water. A netful of solid daphnia was soon gathered and put into the bottom of a 2-pt bait tin together with the powdered aspic and water from the flask. After 20 minutes the mixture was well set. I cut my block of daphnia jelly into ¾ in cubes and slipped one gently on to a size 8 hook. I would love to report that at this point Wilson went on to bag up with 'plump' impossible tench on these daphnia cubes, but I am afraid this is not the case. The wind changed overnight and took with it both tench and daphnia to a distant spot; they were too far away for the cubes to be lowered in, and the super-soft cubes cannot stand up to casting. I had this wonderful idea that all I had to do was lower the cube, which looked exactly what it was, a clear concentration of daphnia, on to the nose of a gorging tench and in it would go. Ah well. It seemed a good idea at the time; and if a similar situation ever arose again, I would go through the same rigmarole.

Opposite: The tench of large clear-water pits and lakes gather wherever the wind and sub-surface tow drifts massive concentrations of daphnia. When gorging themselves close into the margins on these nutritious water fleas, the tench are not distracted even by the continuous passing of water-skiers.

REPRODUCTION

It is the customary close season worry of coarse fishermen throughout England and Wales (no close seasons in Ireland and Scotland, remember) every year as each new season approaches – will the tench have spawned by 16th June or not?

And of course in the vast majority of waters, even shallow lakes and ponds which warm up quickly, they rarely have. In over 30 years of tench fishing I cannot ever remember starting a new season on 16 June at any fishery where the whole tench population had completed its reproduction cycle. There have been isolated years when, due to an incredibly warm spring and more importantly a period of warm nights during late May and early June, which raises water temperatures sufficiently to stimulate spawning, a large percentage of a particular fishery's tench population has indeed shed most of their eggs and milt by mid-June. However, I can only relate to the lake I was concentrating my efforts upon at that time.

Perhaps mother nature has intended that tench should take a long time about reproduction and stagger egg-laying over a period of several weeks regardless of water temperature, to allow for an early lack of soft weed growth, a proponderance of small predators (such as perch), and inclement June weather when sudden over-night frosts dampen everyone's enthusiasm, not just for spawning tench. Besides, the tench species is so incredibly strong (fortunately) that as long as the pot-bellied females are handled carefully, no harm will come to them or their eggs. Nonetheless, I do think that whoever suggested 16 June as an opportune date to end the close season was rather ill advised because in deep, cold gravel pits the tench may not be stimulated into spawning until as late as the end of July. Or were the seasons so very different, say, a hundred years ago? We shall never really know, because most gravel-pit tench fisheries were dug after World War II.

Courtship begins with groups of males, from two up to several at a time, following the females; four or five males all vying for the attentions of a single female is not out of the ordinary. Actual egg-laying sometimes continues throughout the entire day and night, but generally early mornings are chosen. The sudden change in air temperature at that time of day is enough to stimulate a response from the female. She spreads the sticky carpet of eggs through the weeds while the males disperse their milky white milt to fertilize them. As their quiet nature suggests, tench are nowhere near so noisy as carp when propagating their species. They prefer to lay their eggs (unlike carp) in the thickest clumps of soft weeds they can find, and even in the carpets of crunchy, bright green surface algae which dog the surface during summer when water levels are low and there are long periods of bright sunshine.

I remember during the heatwave of 1976, when my brother, David, and I were tench fishing in a large, beautiful, shallow estate lake in North Norfolk, finding by accident thousands upon thousands of 1 to 2 in long tench fry blown to the dam end of the lake amongst the remains of a huge carpet of algae. Unfortunately, the heavy rain which fell continuously throughout that August Bank Holiday weekend had reduced the floating algae almost to nothing. Strangely, the lake contained next to no soft weed beds that year, and the tench had only the algae to use as a spawning cover. What had drawn my attention to the dam end initially was the sight of a large eel gorging itself on surface fry in the shallows by the outlet, which I could see through binoculars from our swim some 100 yd away. When I went to see what was happening I observed more young tench than I have ever seen, either before or since. I rather think most of them fell prey to the eels, perch, and inevitably gulls and herons.

Each female carries an enormous amount of eggs – up to, and even over, one quarter of its body weight – which is why a 9½ lb female can easily tip the scales at over 12 lb when full of spawn. Once the tiny translucent eggs hatch, after 6–10 days, the alevins are initially reliant on yolk from the egg. They then feed on microscopic planktons amongst the weed in which they hide. Anglers may not come into contact with the small tench for at least several years. In most fisheries the young stay in the weed, feeding on minute aquatic life, and rarely come into contact with an angler's bait. From about 1 lb upwards, the tench seems willing to leave the sanctity of weed for long periods and join its larger brethren in small groups, by which time it is liable to suck in food containing a hook.

DISTRIBUTION

Within the British Isles the tench is even more widely spread than carp. While they are not exactly common in Scotland, tench are distributed throughout England and Wales with tremendous concentrations all over Ireland. They have a natural preference for ponds, pits, lakes, meres, broads and reservoirs, but there are few rivers which do not harbour at least a few tench. They are so prolific in the slow-moving Lincolnshire drains and throughout the Great Ouse system, for instance, that a

Comfortably and strategically placed to cover tench as they move through a narrow deep channel connecting one pit to another, this angler offers sweetcorn on the lift rig.

Tench waters come in all shapes and sizes from massive, wind-swept gravel pits where long-range ledgering is often the order of the day, to diminutive, over-grown, secluded lakes where float-fishing beneath the rod tip amongst the lilies offers the best prospects.

good bag of river tench is very likely from any number of locations. Even well-known fast rivers like the Hampshire Avon contain tench, and periodically tench even choose to occupy fast-running areas. Weir pools in particular hold a special attraction during the summer months and whenever the river is in flood. The tench has also been stocked into North American waters and those of Australasia.

CHAPTER THREE

LOCATING TENCH

I HAVE already described how tench give away their position by sending tiny feeding bubbles up to the surface, and a more exact, instant method of locating them does not exist. It is also true to say, however, that even with a fair-sized group of tench packed tightly into a relatively small area, they do not always bubble. It is imperative, therefore, that you know the type of habitats they prefer in various kinds of waters if you wish to catch tench with consistency. Make no mistake: there really is no substitute for learning the craft of observation at the waterside. There is invariably a visual pointer when tench are present, no matter what the conditions, although a situation such as continual really heavy rain can make it difficult to identify. Even on decidedly 'off days', however, when there is little feeling of activity and a complete lack of surface bubbles, there will be a sign or two of tench activity somewhere: reed stalks 'knocking', a sudden but distinctive calm patch amid a rippled surface, the rounded head and shoulders of a tench silently porpoising, patches of discoloured water, rocking lily pads, and so on.

These are just a few of your pointers, so don't forget the binoculars. You will be able to observe things with them that it is not possible to see with the naked eye. Heavy, extremely powerful binoculars are more of a hindrance than a help, because after a while their weight around the neck becomes unbearable, and they spend the rest of the day back in their case. Ideally, you want a lightweight pair with a magnification of 8 × 30 or 10 × 40, which can be hung around the neck all day if required without discomfort. There they are to hand at a moment's notice so that you can observe sudden surface disturbances in soft weed-beds or among lilies, locate sudden eruptions of bubbles beyond the swim being fished, and keep track of

tench should they move on. Binoculars are very much a
working tool and should be used as such. No one should
set off fishing for species like carp, bream and tench, which
portray their presence by surface activity, without them.

It goes without saying that a pair of polaroid glasses are
another indispensable part of the tench fisherman's
armoury. Those with 'yellow' lenses are good because
they polarize and cut out reflective glare from the surface,
and brighten the existing light by a couple of stops. For
dull days, or during periods of low light such as dawn and
dusk, yellow polaroids really are a terrific aid.

STILLWATER HABITATS

Many facets of watercraft are directly linked to location,
and one of the most interesting (for some almost a hobby
in itself) is the study of water plants. As tench are never far
from vegetation when given the choice, locate their
favourite habitats and you have located tench. It's as simple
as that. As small waters such as ponds and pits are a
microcosm of much larger sheets of water, because each
will in fact contain similar features, similar plants, and be
overhung by similar trees, an understanding of the natural
history of ponds and gravel pits will stand you in good
stead for locating tench wherever you fish. For example,
knowledge of the kind of bottom strata preferred by a
particular plant will tell you the nature of the bottom in
that area of water, be it soft or hard.

Reeds

Tall species of grass such as the common reed (often
referred to as the Norfolk reed because it is commonly
used for thatching in that county), which attracts tench like
flies to a honey pot, cannot grow in really soft silt, or it
would soon be uprooted in strong winds. So reeds grow
thickest where the bottom is generally of a firm structure,
such as in gravel, marl or clay.

During the early season the reeds with green, round
stems, which may each grow to 10 ft high, can often be

Find thick beds of the tall common reed lining the margins of a lake, mere, pond or pit and you will have found tench. They can readily be caught on float tackle with the bait presented on the bottom close alongside or actually between small gaps in the reeds.

seen 'twitching', 'clanging' or 'swaying' when there is no wind, as tench either brush the stems as they move between them, or remove crustaceans and aquatic insect larvae such as the caddis grub.

One of my favourite tench waters, Alderfen Broad near Wroxham, has an irregular line of tall reeds along one entire shoreline, and invariably as dawn breaks odd clusters of bubbles can be seen alongside them. To cast a bait between the reeds into bays and narrow channels that reach no further than a couple of feet into the reeds often brings an instant, dramatic response. There is certainly never any dallying. The tench takes the bait with all the confidence in the world and so it should, amongst the reeds it is feeding at home.

Reed mace

Another reed with a liking for a firmish bottom in which to anchor its thick, fibrous roots is the greater reed mace, best known for its large, brown, cigar-like seed heads.

Often called the bullrush (wrongly), the reed mace and the lesser reed mace (a slimmer plant) both attract tench in numbers, particularly during the early season when water temperatures are high. The fibrous-matting type roots at the base are much favoured by spawning tench, which regularly return throughout the following days to mop up their own and the spawn of others.

This angler uses the cover of marginal grasses to present float-fished brandlings alongside the dark, onion-stemmed bull-rushes where tench are working.

Beds of reed mace which make the best tench hot spots are those with their roots in marginal depths of between 2 and 3 ft. Because the stems do not grow so close together as those of the common reed, even large tench may just pass between without so much as a shudder on the brown seed heads. So keep a sharp lookout for tail patterns, or bubbles on the surface amongst the stems.

Bullrush

The true bullrush with its dark green, distinctly onion-like stems, tapering gradually to a fine tip is more commonly found in flowing water. However, it does grow happily in fertile, clear-watered ponds, lakes and pits, where the bottom is guaranteed to attract a prolific colony of freshwater shrimps – and thus tench.

Sweet reed grass

This tall, rush-like marginal prefers a soft bottom where its creeping rootstock form such a dense mass you might be led into thinking you are treading on dry ground, until your boot suddenly fills up. It hangs out over the margins with as much as 3 to 4 ft of water beneath the dark floating canopy, and is much loved by tench. They can be caught directly under the rod tip when patrolling amongst the extensive sub-surface rootstock, which harbours delicacies such as midge larvae, leeches, snails, beetles, caddis and the like.

So much for the more popular 'tench attracting' marginal plants – now let us consider soft weeds and then floating plants.

Soft weeds

These, the submerged oxygenating plants like Canadian pond weed, hornwort, mill foil, can pose enormous problems in clear water where, due to the maximum penetration of sunlight, they grow rampant. And generally speaking the smaller the pond or pit, the more rampant and the more problematic they become. It's often possible to observe bubbles from tench (feeding down on the bottom, beneath the weed) rise to cluster tantalizingly on the surface without there being a way of getting the bait down to them.

Tench are naturally attracted by the overhead protection and diffused light that these soft weeds provide, and of course to the larder of aquatic insect larvae attached to their stems.

To present the bait to tench close into the margins, clear channels or holes need first to be dragged (pp. 81–84), so do not be deterred even about areas that are completely choked and seemingly unfishable. Such swims will (after clearing) allow presentation of the bait on light float tackle, the nicest way of all to catch tench.

Surface plants

Tench love to occupy areas beneath lilies. As for many species, the attraction is a roof over their heads, diffusing the light and obscuring enemies. In such places tench always feel comfortable to browse and feed in their characteristically ponderous, lazy way, even through the heat and brightness of a summer day, when they abandon more open swims as the sun starts to rise high in the sky.

There really is no better day-time retreat in which to locate tench than beneath surface plants. The first 4 lb tench I ever caught came on a bamboo roach pole from beneath surface cover, although the cover was not what you might expect. It did not consist of lilies but an old wooden door (the pit was being back-filled with builders rubble and the like), and from beneath one side of the floating door I could clearly see through polaroid glasses the protruding tails of several large fish. The tails looked in fact to belong to chub, but when I lowered a large lump of flake down beside the edge of the door on a small weightless waggler rig, it suddenly disappeared and I was playing a 4 lb tench which led me a fine song and dance for several minutes on just 3 lb test line. Strangely enough I went on to take a further two tench, both smaller than the first, plus a nice roach from beneath that door, all in an hour's fishing. This illustrates perfectly the value of floating cover, even if the roach pole and fixed line was a trifle cavalierish.

To tackle thick lily beds with inadequate tackle or even the wrong type of outfit (such as a fast-taper rod instead of one with a forgiving, cushioning action) could be asking for trouble. What proves invaluable, however, is an understanding of the structure of stems and roots beneath a mass of floating pads and flowers.

Whilst there are numerous cultivated varieties of coloured lilies available only a handful of clubs or owners plant their fisheries with them. This is a pity because it's impossible to make a stillwater fishery look too beautiful, and to sit catching tench with pink or dark red lilies dotted amongst a carpet of velvet-green pads is a delightful experience.

There are no less than five commonly found 'natural' lily type plants which attract tench: the common yellow

All tench fishermen share a love/hate relationship with soft weeds like the Canadian pond weed. It provides shade above the tench's heads in addition to a larder of aquatic insects, and so encourages clear-water tench to work close into the margins. But in thick beds it creates snags from which it is impossible to extract a hooked tench. There is then only one answer: dragging.

water-lily, sometimes referred to as brandy bottle due to the distinctive shape of the seed head, which forms once the petals have shed; the common white water-lily (the white alba lily); the dwarf pond lily: broad-leaved pond weed; and amphibious bistort.

Tench adore the *common yellow lily* because of its soft, cabbage-like, sub-surface leaves, amongst which they love to browse. Most anglers often refer to this plant simply as 'cabbages', especially in certain river systems where the pads and flowers rarely reach the surface. Boating activity can be responsible for this, as can, to some degree, excessive depth. It is one and the same lily, nonetheless.

The root structure of the common yellow water-lily, with its accompanying sub-surface, lettuce-type leaves, is so enormous and fast-spreading that clubs organize working parties to thin the beds out. Below the mass of surface pads and flowers is a quiet area of diffused light where tench feel at home.

In shallow lakes, however, particularly those with a bottom layer rich in nutrients, the sheer growth of both sub-surface cabbage and floating pads can present a daunting prospect when you are thinking of extracting tench. Nevertheless, present a bait close to or actually amongst the soft leaves, and tench will not be far away.

Second in both size and root structure density to the common yellow lily comes the *white alba lily* and the cultivated hybrids. Due to their very much smaller rhizomes, thinner stalks and complete absence of sub-surface greenery, there is naturally more room beneath the pads and beautiful flowers for tench to both hide and move about, although viewed from the surface the growth looks impenetrable.

The *dwarf pond lily* is not really a true lily, although its small, round green pads and buttercup-yellow flowers would fool most fishermen. The main difference between it and the true lilies (a most useful fact to the tench angler) is that it multiplies rapidly, not by sending up extra stalks and pads from the bottom roots, but by growing outwards

Thick beds of dwarf pond lily help to shade the surface in clear-watered gravel pits, encouraging tench to feed confidently close in along the marginal shelf. This permits simple float-fishing techniques, such as the lift, to be used.

in short bursts across the surface. It creates mini plants each with its own rootstock and flowerhead, every 6–10 in. At the end of the summer these little plants rot off and separate from the old main stem; they drift into the margins where a percentage take hold. And in the following spring, it all sprouts up again. This lily also spreads from the seed head once the yellow flowers die off.

It is by far the fastest-spreading surface plant after duck weed, and it attracts tench in numbers. One advantage of this plant, when you are trying to extract fish from a seemingly impossible surface covering, (see 'Raking') is that while the long stems and pads are tough and thick on the surface, there is little beneath the surface for tackle to catch on. A couple of square yards of floating jungle may be supported underneath by only half a dozen thin stalks.

Broad-leaved pond weed is also regularly frequented by tench. In some locations, especially shallow marl, clay and gravel pits, the oval-shaped green leaves (often noticeably crinkly along the edges) can clog the surface almost from bank to bank. It is easily recognizable by the erect, tight, pink seed heads. Also, from the hard bottom in which it prefers to root, the main stem can sub-divide two or three times before each individual plant reaches the surface. For this reason the density of foliage causes a problem only from mid-water upwards. Like most surface plants, broad-leaved pond weed flourishes best in depths of between 2 ft and 6 ft. This is useful to know when you are reconnoitring new waters, because a reasonably accurate assessment of depths can be made wherever this plant covers the surface.

This applies also to *amphibious bistort* which is really a terrestrial plant that loves to have its roots in water, thus providing a floating canopy for tench in depths up to around 3 ft. It, too, sports an erect, knotty, pink seed head, but the leaves are pointed and dark green. It will occasionally grow as a thick covering well out from the bank over gravel bars, but it is more often seen growing in thick clumps along the margins, sprouting on dry land and reaching out across the surface, exactly where you would expect to find tench browsing.

During the heat of a summer's day, especially when tench feel vulnerable in clear water and are loathe to be seen out in the open, the best place to search is around surface-covering plants.

Hidden sub-surface features

So much for locating tench by visually identifying those plants they most like to frequent, and in part treat as home. But what about lakes, ponds or pits which, for one reason or another, remain weedless for much, perhaps all of the summer – waters without obvious features where the tench might be anywhere. Gravel pits are renowned for their uneven sub-surface contours, created when the sand and gravel deposits were originally laid down following the last Ice Age. To harvest the maximum potential in minerals, aggregate companies dig deeper into the richest seams, thus creating gullies or holes once the pit has been allowed to fill from the water table (fig. 1).

It is along these deeper gullies, or in the holes and drop-offs that tench love to patrol. The bottom lay-out is to them as avenues, cul-de-sacs and road systems appear to us. Obviously, time spent carefully plummetting un-known waters to gain a mental picture of the bottom contours will prevent you wasting time when you are fishing. Make a sketch of each fishery you visit, and draw in the deeper areas so that you have a record for next time.

After spending numerous sessions at a particular pit, it will become obvious that tench frequent certain areas only at certain times of the day. In clear-watered pits, for instance, it usually follows that marginal ledges and gullies are favoured during low light levels such as dusk and dawn, when tench are feeding in earnest on natural food. As the light increases, they evacuate the margins in preference for distant deeps, where they may very well spend all the midday hours. Now this is not a rule of thumb, because tench in each water react differently, but wherever there is a complete lack of marginal cover or surface habitats, such as partly submerged overhanging trees or lily-type plants, it is a good yardstick.

Featureless waters

In featureless waters which appear not to contain definite feeding areas or routes, location is purely one of attraction, as is the case with similar species such as bream. In other

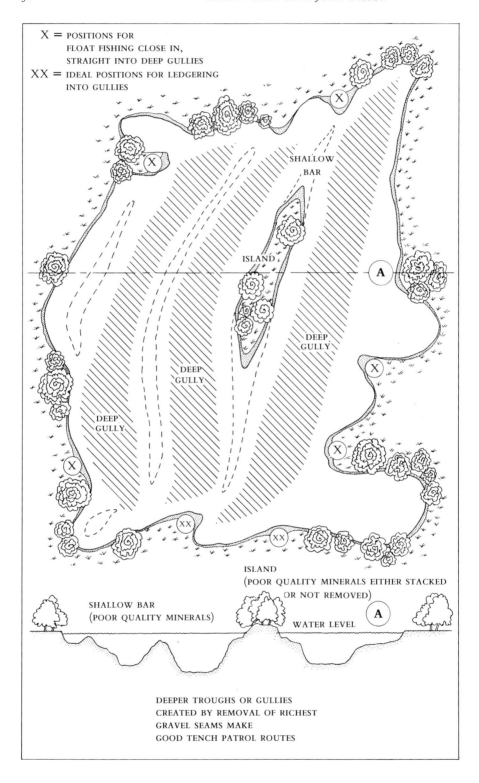

X = POSITIONS FOR
FLOAT FISHING CLOSE IN,
STRAIGHT INTO DEEP GULLIES

XX = IDEAL POSITIONS FOR LEDGERING
INTO GULLIES

SHALLOW
BAR

ISLAND

A

DEEP
GULLY

DEEP
GULLY

DEEP
GULLY

XX

XX

ISLAND
(POOR QUALITY MINERALS EITHER STACKED
OR NOT REMOVED)

SHALLOW BAR
(POOR QUALITY MINERALS)

WATER LEVEL

A

DEEPER TROUGHS OR GULLIES
CREATED BY REMOVAL OF RICHEST
GRAVEL SEAMS MAKE
GOOD TENCH PATROL ROUTES

words, tench are best found by attracting them to an area of your choice by regular pre-baiting (pp. 81–84). Carp anglers know only too well how tench respond to regular helpings of free nosh. In waters with low densities of carp, during the early season especially, tench can actually become a nuisance, pinching the loose feed long before the carp ever find it.

RIVER TENCH

Though comparatively few anglers bother specifically with them, tench in slow, deepish lowland rivers offer an interesting and challenging proposition when they are most active throughout the summer months. The odd fish might even turn up in the winter, especially during and immediately after heavy flooding which has the tendency to wake them up. They are, however, considerably more active in moving water during the warmer months. Years ago my favourite early season tipple was following the bream shoals of the Upper Waveney. This necessitated

A new gravel-pit fishery – perhaps a tench water in the making. The drag-line digs deeper when removing the richest mineral seams, leaving long troughs or gullies. Location of these by careful plummeting of the bottom provides the most likely guide to tench feeding areas and patrol routes.

FIGURE 1 (Opposite) *A mature gravel pit seen from surface level and (bottom) a cross section of the same gravel pit showing how gullies and deep holes – the tench patrol routes – are formed*

pre-baiting a couple of likely-looking deep holes on the
bends between the cabbage patches with mashed bread and
bran (half a bucketful) on the night before, in readiness for
a dawn start. And nearly always, a couple of tench would
come to the net first during half light.

If the bream failed completely to show, then up to half a
dozen river tench were on the cards. Those tench would
consume most of the free nosh during the hours of
darkness in the company of quality roach (a big one
happened along occasionally), but unlike the bream would
hang around for quite some time afterwards as though
they were waiting for more. Thus they were always
obliging customers with the dawn chorus.

Had I the presence of mind at that time (I was far more
intent on catching bream) to pre-bait several swims with
mashed bread, each might have attracted a group of tench
by dawn. And by leap-frogging from swim to swim in
true roving fashion, giving each about half an hour, a bag
of river tench would not have been out of the question.

Numerous opportune tench have come my way over the
years from wandering weedy rivers like the Waveney,
especially while chub fishing, using polaroid glasses to
search among the runs. Once the sun becomes too high for
easy, instant chubbing, and eyes can easily pierce the clear
water down to the bottom, the dark, ponderous shape of a
tench can easily be seen, often 'hovering' well off bottom.
Anglers tend to believe that tench spend much of their time
on or very close to the bottom, but this is simply not the
case. Observation at close quarters allows you to study
their behaviour and see the way in which the tench angles
downwards and stands on its head to suck up a bait
presented hard on the bottom.

Like their stillwater counterparts, river tench love to
browse through the soft, cabbage-like leaves of the
common yellow water-lily. They might turn up anywhere,
but are more liable to frequent choice habitats like beds of
lilies. In addition, search deep and weedy mill pools,
overshoot pools, confluences where ditches or sidestreams
join the main flow creating a depression, deep holes on
acute bends, beneath overhanging willows, and so on.
These are the areas to concentrate on.

Curiously, I have also caught tench from the deepest
water beneath fast-flowing weir pools; however, it is very

much quieter down on the bottom and obviously more to their liking. Built to face a fast flow continuously tench are certainly not; conversely, don't be surprised when large baits like a whole lobworm or lump of bread flake intended for bream or chub produces a tench.

WINTER TENCH

In a typical British winter, with occasional falls of snow and stillwaters frozen over during much of the coldest weather, winter tench are not really a worthwhile proposition. Their metabolic rate seems to slow considerably more than that of carp, although where tench share carp fisheries, and so regularly feed on the boilies introduced to keep the carp interested, they are of course far more commonly caught. And during mild spells brought about by mild south-westerly or westerly winds, the odd tench can be expected at some time during the day.

There is a lovely shallow estate lake at Felbrigg Hall in North Norfolk, where I once used to take large bags of specimen winter rudd. It was particularly productive towards the latter part of the season in early March when temperatures were rising, and whenever the stream which feeds the lake and runs through the middle became flooded, artificially colouring the usually quite clear water. Then and only then could winter tench actually be relied upon to show. My brother, Dave, came up to Norfolk from Hertfordshire one weekend on my so-called guarantee of his getting amongst the big rudd, as at that time during a prolonged mild spell they were really feeding in earnest. But all he caught one after another, on a block-end feeder rig baited with maggots, was no less than 13 tench. Now I use the word 'all' with caution, because a bag of 13 tench is lovely at any time. But they were not what Dave had set his sights upon. Incidentally he never did catch a big rudd from the lake.

I use this occasion to illustrate that in the right weather and water conditions combined, winter tench are certainly on the cards, especially from shallow lakes which warm quickly and get them moving about on the look out for food. Simply scale down a bit on summer strengths of line

and hook sizes, and use smaller baits and far less groundbait or loose feed. And be rather more patient when waiting for bites. Otherwise, the techniques and baits do not really change.

Try swims close to habitats which offer some kind of protection, such as overhanging or partly submerged trees, or amongst the rotting roots where summer lily-beds once graced the surface. Tench will still be around there even in winter.

Deep weir pools hold enormous attraction for tench. This plump 4-pounder accepted John's ledgered bread flake in the middle of a roach and bream haul taken during filming of the TV series, Go Fishing, *made on the River Wensum.*

River tench turn up at the most unlikely times. This 3-pounder gobbled up a worm intended for chub in a backwater of Hertfordshire's River Lea, and provided a bonus winter catch for John's brother.

CHAPTER FOUR

TACKLE

WHILE it is true that even quality tench are sometimes landed on the finest tackle used by match
fishermen, an unacceptable proportion come off when this
type of set-up is used. Either the tiny hook pulls out, the
tackle snags up in weed-beds resulting in a break-off, or the
power of the fish snaps the fine hook link. Conversely,
tench of all sizes are regularly taken by carp fishermen on
tackle which is vastly overgunned in relation to them.
Nobody, for instance, could possibly enjoy cranking in a
3 lb tench hooked on a heavy-bomb shock rig and 10 lb or
12 lb test line.

The result of both these situations (either too light or too
heavy tackle), which are common everyday occurrences, is
that the tench is rarely enjoyed to the full by a large
proportion of anglers. I know numerous young carp
fishermen who never have a good word to say about tench
simply because they have never geared their tackle to suit
and fished specifically for them. The fight of any fish,
tench included, can only ever be related to the tackle being
used to subdue it. So please consider carefully the
following pages about tackle choice, and the tench without
question will become a firm summer favourite.

RODS

At a pinch almost any general-purpose fibre-glass match or
float rod of between 11 ft and 14 ft long or ledger rod of
9 ft to 11 ft will suffice for catching tench. Many situations
can be happily tackled with these two, although inevitably
they will not cover every situation.

As with many items of tackle which have been designed
for a specific purpose, rods particularly suited to catching
tench are more desirable and more versatile. And there is a
wonderful choice in lightweight but robust carbon models

which will allow you to control even the largest fish, while permitting full enjoyment from the ensuing fight whatever size the tench happens to be. So let us consider some of the options.

Float rods

For fishing out into deep water or over beds of marginal lilies with lines up to 4 lb and 5 lb test, choose a good-quality, three-piece 13 ft carbon match rod (a 14-footer if most of your tench fishing will be in deep water). Do not get one with an ultra-fine, spliced tip designed for fishing the stick float with ultra-light hook lengths, because inevitably the tip will snap off.

A 'waggler'-style rod, crisp in action for hitting tiny dips of the float, yet with a 'cushioning' bend throughout, is perfect for the job. Those strengthened with wraps of 'kevlar' are highly recommended.

As lines of up to 5 lb may be used, ask the tackle-dealer to suggest a rod which is not unduly thin in the wall thickness. It is far better to settle for one which weighs a shade more, than to be worrying about a super-lightweight model snapping off when you bend into a tench bent on wrapping the line around lily roots.

When contemplating extracting tench on the float from extremely snaggy close-in situations like dense lily-beds or beside the woodwork of submerged willow branches, where the possibility exists of hooking into really large fish on a break or bust tussle, a carbon match rod is definitely not the tool for the job. This is where a two-piece, 12 ft carbon fibre, 'Avon'-actioned specialist rod is required – one with a test curve of around 1¼ lb, so that it will handle lines from 5 lb to 7½ lb comfortably. The test curve of any rod is the pull required to bend the tip of the rod into a quarter circle, measured in pounds. You then simply multiply that figure (1¼ lb) by 5 to arrive at the ideal line strength – 6¼ lb. You then multiply by 4 (5 lb) and then by 6 (7½ lb) to give guidelines to the rod's lowest and highest limits. This is not to say that much lower hook lengths, for instance, cannot be used with such a rod, because when distance fishing in snag-free conditions with less torque on the outfit, you will be able to fish quite fine, even down to, say, a 3 lb hook link.

This youngster is enjoying the fight of a tench hooked at close range using the right rod for the job: a two-piece, all-through-action Avon.

Ledger rods

The very same Avon-actioned carbon rod with a 1¼ lb test curve is the perfect all-round tool to catch tench when freelining or ledgering. For close range work an 11-footer is sufficient; whereas for picking up more line on the strike in order to hit tiny bites at range, say distances of 40 to 50 yd plus, the extra length of a 12-footer can prove beneficial. Fortunately, carbon fibre's inherent 'quick return' is so effective that bites are seldom missed due to the power of the strike failing to reach the hook. Nevertheless, where distances in excess of 60 to 70 yd are involved, and bites are repeatedly missed for no obvious reason, the answer then is to step up to a more powerful

rod (1½ lb or 1¾ lb test curve). Although drastic, such a rod does not bend anywhere near so much on the strike, and therefore pulls more line through the water, setting the hook home firmly. When using a heavier rod, care must really be taken when the tench is almost beaten and is floundering on a short line beneath the rod tip, ready for netting. One last heavy roll on the surface from the fish when you have minimum cushioning in the rod tip might well pull the hook out, or even snap the hook link – so be careful.

When you are ledgering in the conventional way, using either bobbins or monkey climber indicators, and a strong sub-surface tow bellies the line, thus reducing the effectiveness of the strike, you can increase the ratio of bites hit to those missed with a switch to direct or tight-line ledgering using a quiver tip. A quiver tip can be screwed into the tip ring, or you can choose an Avon rod with a built-in quiver tip, the latter being more desirable because it alleviates that 'dead spot' created by the screw-in junction of tip-ring and quiver-tip threads.

The soft glint of early morning sunlight illuminates this matching two-rod set up for catching tench on the feeder from the shallow waters of a large estate lake. Note how high the rods are set above the surface for maximum line pick-up when striking at range.

By cutting the top 20 in from the tip of an Avon blank and sleeving in (from the butt end) approximately the same length of finely tapered, solid-glass donkey top, you can create a wonderful tench tool. An ideal blank is the North Western two-piece, 1¼ lb test curve, carbon Kevlar Avon, which is available in both 11 ft and 12 ft versions. Spare top joints can always be obtained for conversion, resulting in an Avon rod with the choice of both standard ledger and quiver tops. Alternatively, consider investing in a ready-made and purposefully designed 'twin top' specialist rod, such as the Ryobi carbon Avon, which is 11 ft long and comprises both standard and quiver tops.

I have purposefully recommended using rods of 11 ft plus because in most circumstances the extra length provides greater control of tench hooked in or just beyond weed and lily-beds. Shorter rods only make extracting the fish more difficult, because the line cannot be held out as far.

REELS

In general terms any small to medium-sized fixed-spool reel, smooth in operation and preferably running on ball bearings, is ideal for tench whether you are float or ledger fishing. Its main requirements are that it must hold at least 100 yd of 3 lb to 7 lb test line depending on the situation at hand, and be equipped with an extremely sensitive slipping clutch which can be tensioned progressively, as opposed to some which appear only to have two settings. Whether it has a stern drag and skirted spool, or has a front-adjusting slipping clutch does not particularly matter. However, as I always play fish with the slipping clutch I insist that the action be smooth in operation. There is nothing more frustrating than snapping up or ripping the hook from a fine tench because the slipping clutch failed to give line when it should have. For many years I used the tiny Mitchell 308 reel (now unobtainable) because of its super-sensitive clutch, when there was little else on the market from which to choose. Nowadays, however, several manufacturers specialize in small reels with super-sensitive slipping clutches. Those made by Shimano, ABU, Ryobi and Shakespeare in the upper price brackets are particularly recommended.

The advantage of choosing a lightweight carbon rod and especially a small, lightweight, compact reel is that a medium-sized species like the tench actually seems that much larger and that much more of an adversary when being played. And quite simply, as a tench is hardly likely to rip off 50 yd of line in long runs, or be fished for at great distances, a large-capacity, large-format reel is not required.

When float fishing at close range only, my preference is for the uncomplicated centre-pin reel, and the two models I use regularly are the match aerial and the Stanton Adcock. The degree of sensitivity and gentle yet progress-ive drag that can be applied to the rim of the drum on this reel through thumb pressure will always out-do the clutch on any make of fixed-spool or closed-face reel. However, casts of much more than three rod-lengths, especially from overgrown banks, can pose problems to the centre-pin enthusiast. This reel has its limitations too.

LINES

The lines I use for tench fishing range from 2 lb to 6 lb breaking strain, although very occasionally I add a lighter hook length in gin-clear, open-water swims to stimulate bites from really spooky fish. On the other hand, I may also step up to 8 lb test for really big fish in snaggy situations, but this happens very rarely.

Generally speaking I like the control of 3–4 lb test coupled to a match rod when float fishing, and the durability plus safety margin of 6 lb test when ledgering, especially feeder-fishing which is rather risky on anything lighter. Continual distance casting with a heavy feeder puts enormous strain on even the best-quality monofilament line and is foolhardy with anything less than 6 lb test.

Hook lengths of course are invariably lighter, and vary according to the conditions and bait being used at the time. Occasionally I like to use a pre-stretched and consequently much finer hook length when tench are especially shy. A 5 lb-test, pre-stretched mono, for instance, is in diameter little more than a standard 3 lb test, and gives you a great advantage. However, because of the rigours imposed by casting and playing fish, I never use pre-stretched line on the reel.

Tench fishing demands a hard-wearing, abrasion-resistant monofilament line, but also line with a fair degree of elasticity, and for many years I have been satisfied with brands like Sylcast (Sorrel) and Bayer Perlon in mist green. I do, however, follow a simple code. I also change it regularly. The expense is minimal if you purchase line in bulk and keep it stored away from sunlight. Penny-pinching will inevitably cost you lost fish, and terminal rig left on the bottom is a hazard to wildlife.

HOOKS

For virtually all tench fishing requirements, the Drennan chemically-etched, round-bend, straight-eyed, carbon specimen hooks are absolutely ideal. Throughout the entire size range they are relatively light in the wire so as not to overweight the bait, but are forged strongly enough to subdue the biggest tench without springing open.

For those rare occasions when a step down to a light hook link and size 16 or 18 hook is called for, I swap from eyed to the much neater presentation of a spade end hook,

Hooks need to be sharp, forged, and in the smaller sizes exceptionally strong for catching tench. Round-bend, chemically-etched, straight-eyed, carbon specimen hooks are the author's choice.

and choose the Kamasan chemically-etched, round-bend B640 pattern or the Drennan forged-carbon, chub spade-end. Both are strong enough to deal with tench, incredibly sharp, and light enough in the wire to present casters, maggots or very small worms. It you prefer a super-strong, eyed hook for small baits, try the Drennan super-specialist in sizes 16 to 20.

As the light begins to fade over a Norfolk lake, the chances of tench moving close in along the fringe of marginal sedges are greatly increased, as this thoughtful fisher-man has proved.

For those occasions when offering whole lobworms, mussel, a duo of cockles, and so on, when a long-shank hook is preferable, the Mustad O'Shaughnessy 34021 pattern in sizes 10 to 6 fits the bill admirably.

KNOTS

For tying all eyed hooks when fishing for tench, there are only two knots you need bother with. The best and most reliable knot is the mahseer knot (fig. 2A). With some patterns of chemically-etched eyed hooks, however, which

FIGURE 2 *Knots*

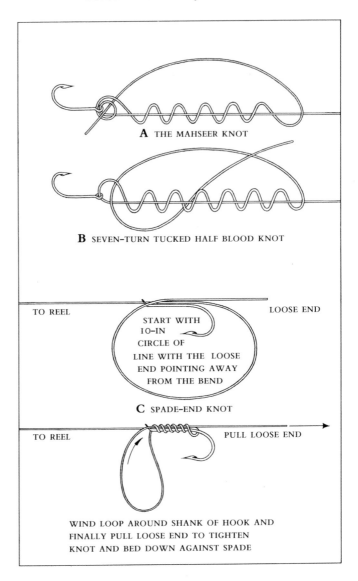

A THE MAHSEER KNOT

B SEVEN-TURN TUCKED HALF BLOOD KNOT

TO REEL   LOOSE END

START WITH
10-IN
CIRCLE OF
LINE WITH THE LOOSE
END POINTING AWAY
FROM THE BEND

C SPADE-END KNOT

TO REEL   PULL LOOSE END

WIND LOOP AROUND SHANK OF HOOK AND
FINALLY PULL LOOSE END TO TIGHTEN
KNOT AND BED DOWN AGAINST SPADE

have a small, extremely neat eye, the end of the line may
not pass through twice. In which case I rely on the seven-
turn, 'tucked' half blood knot (fig. 2B), which is quick to
tie and most reliable. Always remember to wet the line
with saliva before pulling the knot gently tight.

For tying spade-end hooks direct to the reel line or to a
finer hook length, consider the simple knot in fig. 2C,
which requires no threading whatsoever.

To construct a simple fixed paternoster by joining a
hook link to the main line, or for adding a ledger or swim-

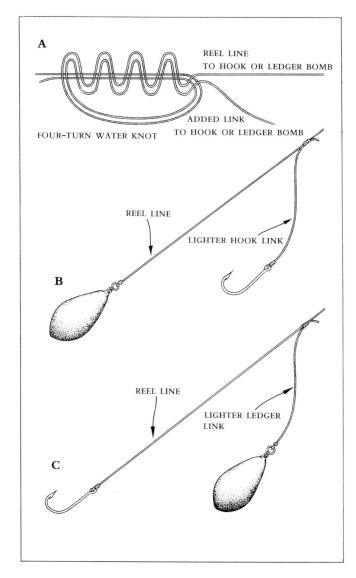

A

REEL LINE
TO HOOK OR LEDGER BOMB

ADDED LINK
TO HOOK OR LEDGER BOMB

FOUR-TURN WATER KNOT

REEL LINE

LIGHTER HOOK LINK

B

REEL LINE

LIGHTER LEDGER
LINK

C

FIGURE 3 *Construct-
ing a simple fixed
paternoster*

feeder link which really will stand away from the main line
to alleviate tangles, there is nothing to beat the four-turn
water knot (fig. 3A). With this simple knot you can safely
tie a light hook link to heavier reel line (fig. 3B), or a thick
bomb or feeder link (so it doesn't tangle) to a finer reel
line (fig. 3C). It is a super knot and particularly neat. It is
also good for joining two lines where the only alternative
is to use a junction swivel, which can pick up weed rather
easily (fig. 4). This problem is alleviated to an extent,
however, by the use of a tiny, lightweight, size 12 barrel

FIGURE 4 *Construct-
ing a fixed paternoster
using a barrel swivel*

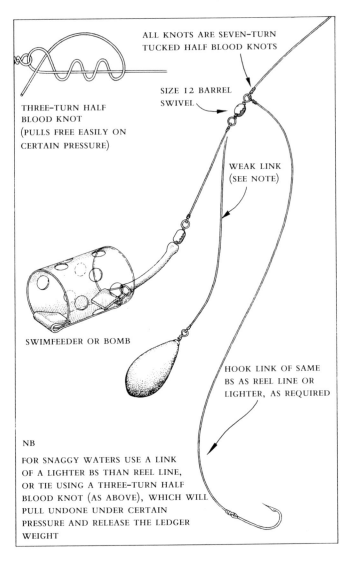

FIGURE 4 *Constructing a fixed paternoster using a barrel swivel*

ALL KNOTS ARE SEVEN-TURN
TUCKED HALF BLOOD KNOTS

SIZE 12 BARREL
SWIVEL

THREE-TURN HALF
BLOOD KNOT
(PULLS FREE EASILY ON
CERTAIN PRESSURE)

WEAK LINK
(SEE NOTE)

SWIMFEEDER OR BOMB

HOOK LINK OF SAME
BS AS REEL LINE OR
LIGHTER, AS REQUIRED

NB

FOR SNAGGY WATERS USE A LINK
OF A LIGHTER BS THAN REEL LINE,
OR TIE USING A THREE-TURN HALF
BLOOD KNOT (AS ABOVE), WHICH WILL
PULL UNDONE UNDER CERTAIN
PRESSURE AND RELEASE THE LEDGER
WEIGHT

swivel, and by tying both hook link and reel line to one
end and the ledger link to the other.

In really overgrown waters where the ledger link may
become snagged while trying to extract a big tench from
weed-beds, I use a weak link or tie just a three-turn half
blood knot, which will pull free at a certain pressure.
Thus, using a junction swivel does have its advantages,
including the option of being able to change the hook link
from long to short or from lighter to heavier quickly
without dismantling the entire end rig, using simple seven-
turn 'tucked' half blood knots.

INDICATORS

As a direct spin-off from the escalation of 'marketed' carp fishing, many newcomers to tench fishing assume that ledgering the bait in conjunction with an electric alarm offers the best indication of biting fish, which is simply not true. Float fishing is way out ahead in terms of sensitivity and in indicating the most delicate of registrations which tench often give.

Floats

For the lift method all you need is a range of straight, commercial peacock wagglers taking from 1BB up to 1 swan shot. If you can obtain them (try the local zoo or wildlife park) unpainted peacock quills with the herl removed, cut into various lengths from 3 in to 10 in are even better. Simply cover one end in ½ in of matt red or orange fluorescent paint, and attach to the line at the opposite end with a ¼ in section of silicone float rubber. This makes the cheapest, most effective float of all.

Incidentally, you should attach commercial wagglers to the line in the same way if presenting the lift method, *not* with the line threaded through the bottom ring and locked on either side by bulk shot. The lift rig is only effective when the shots are close to the hook.

In addition to straight peacock quill/wagglers, a range of bodied wagglers or drift-beater floats, which have greater shotting capacity, are useful for fishing at distance or in choppy conditions. Not all the mornings when you float-fish for tench will be flat calm and misty.

At the other end of the scale, a range of extremely delicate stillwater antenna floats, possessing extra-fine tips to indicate the merest suggestion of a tench closing its lips over the bait, will also come in handy.

Coil indicators

When freelining large baits such as the insides of a whole medium-sized, freshwater swan mussel, or a couple of lob worms, all you require on the line between butt ring and

reel is a simple coil indicator. These can be made by cutting
1 in diameter plastic piping into 2 in segments, finishing
with a horizontal cut so that each clips easily over the line.
Or by folding two or three layers of silver kitchen foil into
1–2 in wide strips several inches long, and hanging over
the line in a coil. An electric alarm used as the front rod
rest ahead of the coil as an early warning indicator is
optional.

Bobbins

Whether it is used in conjunction with an electric bite
alarm or simply clipped on the line by itself between butt
ring and reel, the basic hair-grip type bobbin is the most
sensitive of all visual indicators. These are obtainable in
dayglo colours, or in clear plastic enclosing luminous
betalight elements, which last for 15 years and suffice for
both daytime and night fishing. Of the various makes
available, the 'Glo Bobbin' is best of all. I have used them
for over 10 years and the betalights still work. However,
the luminosity of betalight elements reduces at somewhere
between 5 to 10 per cent per year. It is a simple matter to
replace them using elements of around 250–300 micro-
lamberts (the strength in which luminosity is rated), which
are quite bright enough to see when you are sitting mere
feet away from the rods.

For connecting the bobbin to the front rod rest do not
use heavy-gauge monofilament, which only twists and
clangs back when the bobbin departs from the line as you
strike. Go for around 2½ ft of old fly line which, due to its
lack of stretch, never tangles and permits the bobbin to
drop harmlessly to the ground on the hardest of strikes. To
the rod-rest end of this retaining line I attach a large
American snap swivel. This easily and quickly clips on to a
tiny ring (the sort used as hook retainers on fly rods)
whipped on to the rod rest (see fig. 5). This process may
sound like a rigmarole, but it is well worth the effort for
convenience sake if you are using bobbin indicators
regularly.

I much prefer clip-on bobbins when ledgering for
species such as bream, roach and tench, as opposed to the
more modern monkey climbers, because I wish to be able

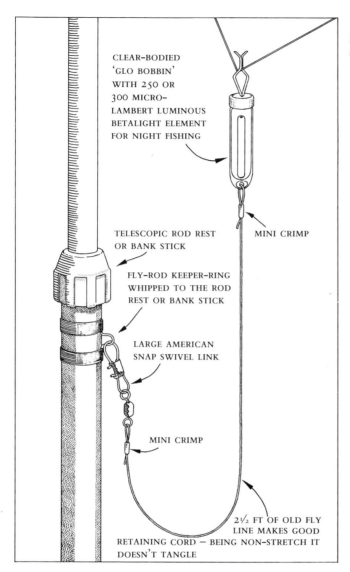

CLEAR-BODIED
'GLO BOBBIN'
WITH 250 OR
300 MICRO-
LAMBERT LUMINOUS
BETALIGHT ELEMENT
FOR NIGHT FISHING

TELESCOPIC ROD REST
OR BANK STICK

MINI CRIMP

FLY-ROD KEEPER-RING
WHIPPED TO THE ROD
REST OR BANK STICK

LARGE AMERICAN
SNAP SWIVEL LINK

MINI CRIMP

2½ FT OF OLD FLY
LINE MAKES GOOD
RETAINING CORD – BEING NON-STRETCH IT
DOESN'T TANGLE

FIGURE 5 *Bobbin indicator set-up*

to see the very tiniest indication of a bite. With a bobbin clipped on to the line between butt ring and reel this happens, provided it hangs vertically down immediately below the butt ring. If a fish moves the bait 6 in the bobbin will rise 6 in, as in fig. 6A. If it is suspended midway between butt ring and reel (fig. 6B) it will register a reduced bite. This is because the line slides through the bobbin clip as the bobbin moves, the bobbin can only rise half that distance – just 3 in.

This is exactly what happens when a monkey climber

FIGURE 6 *Why the hanging bobbin indicator is best*

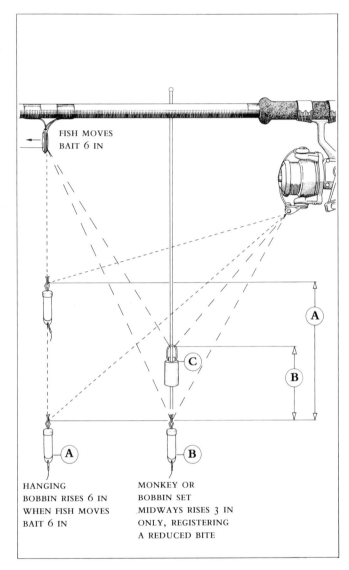

FISH MOVES
BAIT 6 IN

A

C

B

A

B

HANGING
BOBBIN RISES 6 IN
WHEN FISH MOVES
BAIT 6 IN

MONKEY OR
BOBBIN SET
MIDWAYS RISES 3 IN
ONLY, REGISTERING
A REDUCED BITE

indicator is positioned where it operates at its smoothest – midway between butt ring and reel (fig. 6C) – giving a reduced bite indication every time, equal to only half the distance the fish moved the bait. When tench provide positive bite indications, this is perhaps not so worrying, but there are times when I expect to hit mere ¼ in movements of the bobbin, whether up or down. After all, if a float with ¼ in of its tip visible above the surface suddenly vanished, it would be considered a good bite. Ledgering indicators should work on the same basis.

A sensibly arranged two-rod set-up using ledger bobbins in conjunction with Optonic bite indicators. The ideal combination for attacking distant swims when float-fishing is impractical.

To counteract wind drift or a strong underwater tow which slowly pulls the line and raises the bobbin, simply pinch one, two or even three swan shot on the retaining cord immediately below the bobbin.

Monkey climbers

When used in the best position for the monkey to rise freely (i.e., suspended midway between butt ring and reel) this indicator can only move half the distance the bait has been pulled by the tench. When fishing in gale force winds, however, because the indicator is held on a needle and does not swing about (like a bobbin), the monkey climber has an advantage over other methods.

The 'grease monkies' manufactured by Gardner Tackle, with black, PTFE-coated, stainless steel needles and segmented bodies which can be made 'lighter' or 'heavier', are really excellent. There is a vertical hole in the main body for the insertion of a betalight for night fishing.

BITE ALARMS/BUZZERS

Whether freelining and using a silver foil indicator or ledgering with a bobbin set up, reliance on the piercing call of an antenna or optonic type buzzer to jar the brain into immediate action certainly puts a lot more tench on the bank. Bite alarms allow you, with the help of binoculars, to capitalize on what's happening in other parts of the fishery where the tench are moving, or to relax and delight in the sights and sounds of the natural history. At a moment's notice, it's possible to turn around and instantly focus your attention – and striking arm – on the indicator (if using a two-rod set up), which rises or falls as the alarm shrieks its warning.

Optonic bite indicators

I can relate to this particular alarm, which is also a bite indicator, more easily than all others. For every $\frac{3}{4}$ in of line which travels across the sensitive, frictionless wheel, a single bleep tone plus warning light is emitted, which means that instantly I know whether the bite is a mere twitch, a slow run, or a fast run – and can react accordingly. For example if there are numerous tench in a confined, shallow weedy area and the bobbin 'jingles' every so often because a fish bumps into the line registering a single bleep I gear my mind to ignore these 'liners' and respond only to more positive indications. On other occasions, however, when bites are few and far between, I may strike instantly at a single bleep identifying it as a diminutive bite, especially if, having ignored previous single bleeps, I have reeled in afterwards to find that the maggots or corn have been sucked to skins.

The Optonic works only when the line moves forwards

or backwards (as in a drop-back bite). The moving line rotates a tiny fan-blade on the wheel spindle, either side of which is a photo-electric cell. When the indicator is switched on these two cells are connected by an invisible beam of light. Whenever the light beam is interrupted by the fan, the indicator bleeps. It is so simple yet devastatingly effective, and is available in various self-contained, cordless compact models, with or without volume and tone control. In some models the sensor heads are connected by wires to a sounder box, which can be positioned several yards away. It was on a tench fishing trip that I reviewed the Optonic indicator when it first became available and took the tackle trade by storm in 1978. I caught a fair bag of tench that day under difficult conditions too, many of them due to the indicator's effectiveness and I have forgotten how many hundreds of tench it has accounted for since.

The only drawback, and some might say it creates an unacceptable disturbance to the peacefulness and tranquillity of beautiful tench lakes and pits, is that a large proportion of anglers will insist on informing every other angler about the number of bites they are having by turning the Optonic's volume control up far too loudly.

I am often asked why it is that I rarely use buzzer bars which allow for two (or more) Optonics to be neatly assembled on a single telescopic bankstick or butt rest. I like to have the option of being able, within seconds, to angle one rod in a completely different direction to the other (something which is not possible with buzzer-bar set-ups); for example, to cover a tench which has just rolled or to place a bait over rising bubbles, both of which could happen well away from the baited area. The back rests are not disturbed; I simply pull the front one out and reposition it so the rod is in a direct line with the point where the bait is to be cast. It means carrying four telescopic bank sticks about instead of two, or course, but to my opportunist mind it is well worth the effort.

Incidentally, if you intend doing a fair amount of ledgering for tench using bite indicators, it is well worth investing in good-quality bank sticks with solid points for working easily into hard gravel and sensible locking collars for quick height adjustment. Those made of stainless steel are particularly recommended.

The audible indication of a bite alarm allows you to relax while ledgering for tench in large open waters, and to capitalize on what is happening in other areas. Search the surface with bin-oculars for signs of the tench's presence, and you may catch bonus fish.

SUNDRIES

Landing-nets

As few tench exceed a length of 24 in, a landing-net of that size with either a triangular or round frame is more than adequate. Size for size, my preference will always be for the round frame, because it provides more netting area (fig. 7).

I also like a deep 24 in twin-mesh net which has minnow-mesh sides and a flat, micromesh bottom upon which the tench gently rests for unhooking without small shots or bombs slipping through and tangling. Weighing a shade over 1lb when wet, this net is also tailor-made for weighing the tench without going to all the bother of wetting a specialized weigh sling and moving the fish from one to the other. You simply unscrew the landing-net pole and hoist net frame plus tench onto the scales, remembering to deduct the net frame afterwards. To permit netting of tench caught around reed stems or amongst lilies well out

For netting tench of all sizes, a round, 24 in diameter frame fitted with a deep, twin-mesh net screwed into a long, telescopic fibreglass handle is perfect.

FIGURE 7 *The ideal-sized landing-net: 24 in round frame*

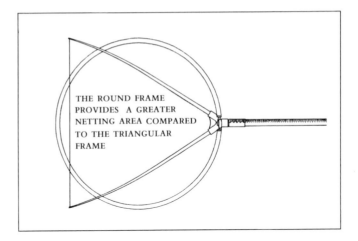

THE ROUND FRAME
PROVIDES A GREATER
NETTING AREA COMPARED
TO THE TRIANGULAR
FRAME

from the bank, I use the longest telescopic glass landing-net pole that I can comfortably wield.

Keep-nets/sacks

Having used both soft nylon sacks and micro-meshed keep-nets for well over a decade, I am still undecided as to which is more suitable for the purpose and less harmful to the fish. I suspect that both are tench friendly, and that being dark and soft the fish lie quiet inside, without having their protective layer of body mucus removed. And so, depending on convenience, I shall continue to use both and recommend the reader enjoys the same choice.

The main point to consider is that wet keep-nets are heavy to carry at the end of a session. If you have a long walk from the car when fishing a lake that rarely produces more than one or two tench per session, then the easily portable sack is the obvious choice. If you are parked close to a swim where a big bag of tench is on the cards, a large micro-mesh net somewhere between 10 and 12 ft long and with a 20 in diameter is the best choice.

Unhooking mats

The foam-lined unhooking mats used for carp fishing, which protect the fish whenever the banks are unfriendly as many gravel pit fisheries are, work wonderfully well with tench. If you purchase a large mat at the outset, it will suffice for carp, pike, and medium-sized species such as bream and tench. Do not, however, take the tench out of the landing-net and lie it on the unhooking mat. Simply lower the net on to the mat and use the wet mesh for holding the tench in your left hand while unhooking it with your right. The tench can then be lowered straight back into the water, or in to the top of the keep net, and the landing-net reversed to free the fish with the minimum of handling.

Weed rakes/drags

If you are committed, either through lack of transport or local choice, to tench fishing in extremely weedy fisheries, some sort of weed-clearing device is essential if you wish to continue fishing throughout the summer.

Rakes or drags designed specifically for the angler are not manufactured, but it is not difficult to make your own. For years tench fishermen have been wiring together (use 20 gauge galvanized wire) the steel heads of two garden rakes back to back, and tying on a long length of

FIGURE 8 *Home-made weed rake*

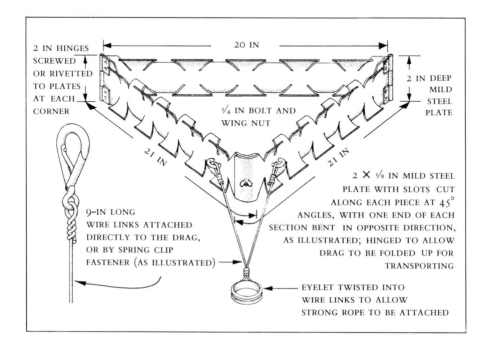

2 IN HINGES SCREWED OR RIVETTED TO PLATES AT EACH CORNER

20 IN

2 IN DEEP MILD STEEL PLATE

¼ IN BOLT AND WING NUT

21 IN

21 IN

2 X ⅛ IN MILD STEEL PLATE WITH SLOTS CUT ALONG EACH PIECE AT 45° ANGLES, WITH ONE END OF EACH SECTION BENT IN OPPOSITE DIRECTION, AS ILLUSTRATED; HINGED TO ALLOW DRAG TO BE FOLDED UP FOR TRANSPORTING

9-IN LONG WIRE LINKS ATTACHED DIRECTLY TO THE DRAG, OR BY SPRING CLIP FASTENER (AS ILLUSTRATED)

EYELET TWISTED INTO WIRE LINKS TO ALLOW STRONG ROPE TO BE ATTACHED

'throwing' rope securely in the middle. This makes a cheap and most efficient tool for pulling out dense lilies or other surface plants and for removing rampant soft weeds such as Canadian pond weed or mill foil.

During the winter months there is no better time for constructing your own designer weed drag. An excellent pattern (fig. 8) handed down to me by my old friend Bill Cooper of Norwich has, over the years, proved to be most useful. It is light, well worth the trouble to make, and really cleans out a swim fast, whatever it happens to be clogged with.

Alternatively, it's well worth scanning the tool section at your local garden centre, where a range of interesting and useful rakes and rake heads of every conceivable description are available at a price.

CHAPTER FIVE

BAITS

IF my tench fishing was limited to the use of just one bait, I would find it difficult to choose between bread flake, worms and sweetcorn. Fortunately there is no such restriction, and I can enjoy using and experimenting with a whole variety of baits to suit the situation at hand, from the humble shop-bought maggot to designer milk protein pastes. In recent years, tench which previously only saw the more conventional, commonly-used baits at the start of each new season, are now bombarded with every carp bait ever invented. And once they have learnt to accept baits such as boilies and the popular particles like peanuts or black-eyed beans as natural food, because they are so regularly introduced into the water, tench acquire a genuine taste for them.

Wherever tench share a fishery with carp, it is as well to accept that if any amount of pre-baiting has taken place with particles or boilies, then these baits could indeed outfish the old standbys like maggots, worms and corn. So don't bang your head against a brick wall. If the tench want boilies, let them have boilies. Tench also respond well to attractor baits such as tares and hempseed, which again were probably used initially to attract carp into the margins, but which eventually draw more and more tench into the area.

Tench are noticeably attracted by all mass baits such as corn, casters and maggots, because their natural staple diet of bloodworms (midge larvae) abounds in the silt by the million. They are therefore not so alarmed by them as they might be by the sight of a large piece of bread flake sitting on the bottom. Although perhaps this is unfair, because bread is one of the most effective baits for tench.

At the end of the day there is no best bait for tench, or indeed for any fish. It is a case of trial and error. So let us explore the tench fisherman's potential armoury, starting with naturals, where fishing baits first began, with worms and the garden fork.

NATURALS

Worms

Few other baits are treated with the same aggression or instigate such positive bites as worms. I rate lobworms extremely highly as a specimen tench bait whatever the conditions, and especially during windy weather and in low water temperatures when tench generally are not responding.

To make a large ledgered lobworm gyrate attractively several inches above the bottom weed, inject a little air into the head with a hypodermic syringe. Be very careful when doing this, however, because if the needle slips and you accidentally inject air into your finger, the result could be fatal. Lobworm sections threaded up the shank and topped with a couple of maggots or a single grain of corn work well, too.

You should never set off tench fishing without brandlings, those yellow-banded wrigglers found in manure heaps. Few naturals have such instant pulling power as brandlings presented two or three up on a size 12 or 10 hook, topped with a single maggot so they cannot wriggle off over the barb. Whenever there is enough to go round, catapult a few fragments of chopped worms, lobs or brandlings, into the swim around the float, or mix them into the groundbait for throwing or catapulting out while ledgering.

Mussels

Next to the bloodworm, there cannot be a more natural bait to offer the tench than the freshwater swan mussel. Nearly every stillwater and even fast-flowing rivers abound with this mollusc, which always grows to its largest (often exceeding 6 in in length) in the mineral richness of the siltiest lakes and pits. They live with their shell part-buried in the detritus, feeding and breathing by continually syphoning water through their system. They do in fact move rather more quickly than one would imagine, with a keel-like foot protruding from the bottom corner of their blunt end. In thick silt they leave behind a definite furrow.

Gather mussels by pulling a long-handled garden rake along the bottom through the margins. Some areas will be far more prolific than others, so don't despair if you are not immediately successful. In really muddy or silty shallows, it's just as easy to roll your sleeves up and feel for them. They can easily be kept alive for several days in a bucket of water, but soon die and go off when left dry.

To open the clam-like shell do not try and prize it apart with your fingers. It fractures surprisingly easy, and the jagged edges are capable of inflicting a nasty wound. Enter the shell with a thin-bladed knife and sever the powerful hinges at each end, whereupon it will open readily. Tench adore the large, orange-coloured, meaty insides, whether presented whole on a size 4, or chopped into smaller chunks. Many a tench angler has struck a confident run on whole mussel, only to find that a specimen rudd or roach was the greedy culprit. Do not worry about what appears to be an oversize bait; it easily folds and gets sucked in by those rubbery lips. Whole mussels are best freelined (p. 85), resulting in the most positive runs you are ever likely to encounter from a tench. Pre-bait for a few days, scattering the chopped-up insides of, say, a dozen mussels into a favourite known tench swim. Then try one on the hook.

Cockles

Whether tench respond eagerly to cockles because the orange meat reminds them of a baby swan mussel, I cannot say. However, following a few days of pre-baiting, cockles will have tench climbing up the rod – or they will produce absolutely no interest at all.

Buy them in bulk ready-boiled from the fishmongers, and separate into smaller batches in polybags before popping into the freezer for later use. Prior to freezing, they can be coloured with the same powder dye used in making carp baits. Simply add a teaspoonful of dye to half a cupful of hot water and pour over the cockles in a 2 pt bait tin. Colour the cockles in 1 pt batches, stirring gently until they are evenly coloured, then strain off excess dye before freezing.

Tench have a distinct preference for the smell of natural baits. Worms, especially brandlings, are at the top of the list.

Tench love the aroma of natural baits. When you find it impossible to collect a fresh batch of lobworms from the lawn after dark, both prawns and cockles are worth trying instead.

Prawns and shrimps

Again, these are most cheaply bought in bulk (several pints
at a time) from the fishmongers ready boiled and peeled.
Split them into separate batches for freezing. As with
cockles, pre-baiting over a period of several days will
allow the tench to acquire a liking for the succulent meat,
which is best presented beneath a float lift style (p. 88).
Long casting is rather risky as the soft meat tears easily and
will fly off in mid air.

Maggots

These are a fine tench bait, though being the most
commonly-used bait of all, their effectiveness quickly
wears off once tench start to become suspicious of them. It
is then a case of reducing both hook and line size until
tench feel confident in sucking the maggot or maggots in,
which is not really a satisfactory situation in heavily
weeded waters. So whilst they are among the first choice
in baits with which to commence the new season, don't
prolong their use when bites slow up.

Maggots that have been dyed red seem to have the edge,
perhaps because they then become associated with bloodworm by the tench.

Casters

These are rated by many keen tench fishermen as a more
productive bait than maggots. Certainly their presence in
groundbait really gets the tench rooting about, especially if
all the juices are squeezed out of the casters and mixed into
the groundbait. It seems to add that extra inexplicable
'something'.

Casters are great presented singly on a size 16, or two
and three up on a size 14 or 12. However, they are even
more effective in a 'cocktail' with sweetcorn, brandlings or
red maggots. When fishing over heavy bottom-weed, two
dark (buoyant) casters will suspend a size 14 hook nicely
just on top of the weed.

PARTICLE BAITS

Sweetcorn

Of all the particle baits that attract tench, sweetcorn is by far the most effective, whether ledgered or float-fished. One piece on a size 14 is about right, or three up on a size 12 or 10. It all depends on the size of the kernels. Tinned sweetcorn tends to be noticeably smaller (and more expensive) than the frozen variety.

For presenting a really good mouthful when tench are spitting out the skins without registering a bite, simply thread two or three kernels up and over the eye of a size 8 hook onto the line above. Then slip three kernels on to the hook and slide the others gently back down again. It works wonders.

On heavily fished waters, sweetcorn's effectiveness is reduced because everyone tends to rely on its pulling power, particularly early in the season. In this case, terminal tackle must be scaled down if you wish to stay catching on corn. It is not that the tench stop eating it; far from it, all the loose feed certainly gets mopped up. They simply become suspicious of corn on the hook. You then have three choices. Rig up a short hair and present it off the hook. Change its colour from yellow to red or orange (using a powder carp bait dye), or stop using it and change to another bait.

Stewed wheat

This is easy to prepare, and is a great follow-on or alternative particle to sweetcorn. Put a few pints into a plastic bucket with a rip-off lid, cover by at least several inches of boiling water (to allow the grains to expand fully), and push the lid on firmly. Within a few hours the excess water can be strained off, and the succulent kernels, with their distinct 'nutty' aroma, can be separated into batches and popped into the freezer for later use.

You can dye stewed wheat red, purple or orange by adding powder dye to the boiling water. Give this bait a good try. Tench love it, and you can purchase a sack of wheat for a few pounds.

Hempseed and tares

Although tench are caught with these particles presented on the hook, I think of them more as attractor baits, to be scattered or catapulted either as loose feed or mixed into the groundbait, whilst using other 'larger' baits on the hook. Prepare them overnight in boiling water as for stewed wheat, and then leave for a couple of days for the seeds to ferment in their own juices. Don't worry about the smell, tench love it.

Beans, peas and nuts

Beans such as haricots, black eyed beans, red kidney beans, chickpeas and peanuts do not have the 'instant' tench appeal of maggots, worms, bread or sweetcorn. However, they are all effective particle baits in fisheries where they have been exhaustively used to attract carp, and where eventually the tench have also learnt to accept them as food. For 'carp-orientated' tench, black-eyes and peanuts especially seem to be favoured. They may be float-fished lift style (p. 88), on or off a hair, and ledgered bolt-style (p. 121) either side-hooked or on a hair. The permutations on any particular water are as endless as for carp fishing.

Boilies

As I have already mentioned, boilies are very popular with tench in fisheries which have been heavily pre-baited to attract carp. By the same token, after several pre-baiting sessions boilies will also catch tench on waters where carp do not exist, but where most standard tench baits like worms, paste, maggots, and soft particles are ripped to pieces by hoards of small nuisance fish such as perch, roach or rudd.

Once the tench (like carp) become suspicious of the standard, side-hooked boilie (fig. 9A), thread them off the hook on to a fine hair (fig. 9B). This gives the tench greater confidence when sucking them up, and conse-quently produces more bites. Shock or bolt rig tactics are

Probably the most instant tench bait ever used, sweetcorn can be offered in a good mouthful by threading three kernels onto the line and sliding them up against another three on the hook.

Be forever willing to experiment by varying bait combinations when bites are not forthcoming. A cocktail of sweetcorn that has been dyed red and maggots led to the downfall of this lovely fish.

not necessarily required. Boilies work well presented in the lift style beneath a buoyant peacock quill (see Lift method, p. 88), and on a standard feeder rig (see 'Ledgering' p. 108). When these and all other avenues fail to produce hittable bites, the time has arrived to present the boilie bolt-style. Most respectably-sized tench can easily manage 14 mm to 18 mm boilies, but they do show a marked preference for 8 mm to 10 mm mini boilies. The yellow minis produced by Richworth (Honey Yukatan), probably owing to their colour and similarity in size to sweetcorn, are worth trying first. You can then ring the changes through the difficult colours and flavours, moving on to larger boilies as the situation dictates.

A comprehensive selection of baits suitable for a day's feeder fishing – hook offerings of red and yellow sweetcorn, brandlings, bread, casters, maggots and boilies, plus slightly dampened bread crumbs for plugging each end of the feeder.

Best colours overall seem to be yellow, red and orange, while either very sweet or seafood flavours are the best attractors. Try pre-baiting with mini boilies but using a 14 mm one on the hook so it really stands out. Or pre-bait with tares or hempseed and fish a mini boilie on the hook. There are countless permutations with which to experiment.

FIGURE 9 *Hooking boilies*

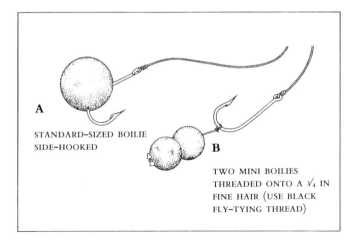

A

STANDARD-SIZED BOILIE
SIDE-HOOKED

B

TWO MINI BOILIES
THREADED ONTO A $\frac{1}{4}$ IN
FINE HAIR (USE BLACK
FLY-TYING THREAD)

PASTES

Soft protein pastes

The same milk-based protein ingredients as are used in boiled baits, mixed with water, flavouring and colouring, make exceptionally fine paste baits for tench. If you like to make your own boilies give yourself a treat and save yourself time by using your favourite recipe as a soft paste, just as it is prior to being rolled into balls and boiled. The main reason for boiling is to produce a protective skin around the bait which irritating, unwanted species cannot pick at (boilies were first created for carp, remember). So if your tench lake is not rampant with shoals of paste-nicking shoal fish, allow the tench to sample large soft paste baits either float-fished, freelined or ledgered.

A piece of paste the size of a 50 p coin, covering a size 6 hook and flattened so it flutters slowly down and settles gently on top of any soft weed, is absolutely ideal. To pre-bait, introduce a few dozen paste pieces into several adjoining swims (so all the local tench see them) every other day over a period of a week or two. Then start using them on the hook. You could be amazed at the pulling power of soft paste. To make the paste really buoyant, so it rests ever so gently on top of weed, use a couple of ounces of sodium casenate in the base mix. A good formula to start with is equal proportions (say 4 oz each) of calcium casenate, wheatgerm, lactopro and soya isolate, plus water and your choice of flavour and powder colouring, all kneaded together to produce a soft but slightly rubbery texture. Tench do tend to shy away from white (uncoloured) pastes – possibly it reminds them too much of white bread flake, on which they may have been repeatedly caught in the past.

Trout pellet paste

This evil-smelling khaki-coloured paste, a concoction of fish meals and grains, will really get tench going. It is available in pellet form, and you can either break it down to dust in a coffee-grinder (a handful at a time), then add warm water and knead into a paste, adding wheat gluten or cornflour to bind; or dampen the pellets liberally with hot water and wait an hour or so before kneading and adding the binders.

A favourite old carp recipe which tench adore is to add a spoonful or two of phillips yeast mixture (a bird tonic available from pet shops) to the pellet paste.

Trout pellet paste is best freelined or ledgered, but like all baits can be presented beneath a float. For loose feed, scatter in some pellet mash (to which extra water has been added so it clouds the swim) around your hook bait. When using pellet mash, you will need an old towel for wiping your hands.

Bread paste

Bread paste is considered rather old hat, but its creamy consistency will attract tench from a great many waters. For the best paste you need old bread. Give it a good soaking, and squeeze out all the excess water; then knead it thoroughly into a firm yet pliable paste.

It can be coloured (use powder dye), and it may be flavoured with liquid essences. It fact, all sorts of additives can be included. Finely grated cheddar cheese used 50/50 with bread paste, plus a spoonful of marmite, makes a fabulous tangy bait; it can be fozen and used at any time. Alternatively, try sausage-meat, again used 50/50 with bread paste, with additives like marmite, bovril or a crushed oxo cube kneaded in.

The orange insides of a freshwater swan mussel, which abound in the mud or among the gravel shallows of most lakes and pits, make a fine natural bait for tench. Freeline on a size 4 hook tied direct to 5 or 6 lb line.

Sausagemeat

This is a very effective bait, especially in heavily-coloured waters. It can be used just as it is with a little cornflour added to stiffen it into a paste.

Cooked sausages also tempt tench. Any type – pork, beef, spicy, or frankfurthers straight from the tin – can be cut into ½ in cubes, which suffices for both loose feed and hook baits. And I dare you to go tench fishing with a bag of sausage cubes without eating a few.

Tinned meats like that good old standby, luncheon meat (always carry a tin in the tackle bag), may be cut into oblongs or cubes of any size. For particularly spooky tench they are best presented on a fine hair rig.

Luncheon meat

No tackle bag or car boot should ever be without a tin of luncheon meat or two. This bait should be standard issue to every young angler with his first rod and reel outfit. Don't be fussy about brands. Simply cube the meat with a long-bladed, very sharp knife, ensuring that the cubes measure exactly the length of the hook. That way,

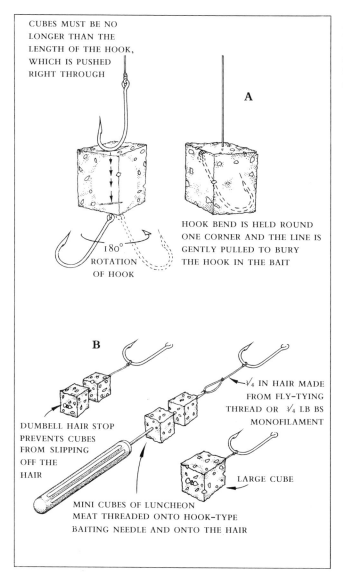

CUBES MUST BE NO LONGER THAN THE LENGTH OF THE HOOK, WHICH IS PUSHED RIGHT THROUGH

A

180° ROTATION OF HOOK

HOOK BEND IS HELD ROUND ONE CORNER AND THE LINE IS GENTLY PULLED TO BURY THE HOOK IN THE BAIT

B

DUMBELL HAIR STOP PREVENTS CUBES FROM SLIPPING OFF THE HAIR

¾ IN HAIR MADE FROM FLY-TYING THREAD OR ¾ LB BS MONOFILAMENT

LARGE CUBE

MINI CUBES OF LUNCHEON MEAT THREADED ONTO HOOK-TYPE BAITING NEEDLE AND ONTO THE HAIR

FIGURE 10A *Hooking on luncheon meat and B hair-rigged luncheon meat cubes*

hooking on meat will never pose a problem. Simply push the hook through the middle of the cube (fig. 10A) until you can grip the bend with your fingernails, and pull through. Then push the point and bend around a corner and gently pull on the line. The hook will be completely hidden, yet will cut through the meat immediately on the strike. Luncheon meat cubes (and sausage cubes) can, of course, also be threaded on to a hair, using a couple of mini cubes or one large one (fig. 10B).

BREAD

Last but not least, don't forget the pulling power of good, old-fashioned breadflake. Used in large lumps on size 6 or 8 hooks, breadflake has the uncanny knack of producing the larger tench. It is also effective, for finicky fish, presented on much smaller hooks, as is a small cube of breadcrust. Crust is very effective in swims that are heavily carpeted in soft weed; its inherent buoyancy means that it is always visible. A small piece of crust threaded up the shank of a size 10 hook with a couple of casters or maggots on the bend makes an electric cocktail. All sorts of combinations are worth persevering with (fig. 11).

FIGURE 11
Combinations and cocktails when using bread

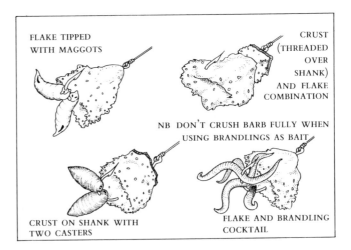

FLAKE TIPPED WITH MAGGOTS

CRUST (THREADED OVER SHANK) AND FLAKE COMBINATION

NB DON'T CRUSH BARB FULLY WHEN USING BRANDLINGS AS BAIT

CRUST ON SHANK WITH TWO CASTERS

FLAKE AND BRANDLING COCKTAIL

GROUNDBAITS

In certain situations, such as fishing waters low in stocks of tench but where individual fish run to specimen proportions, groundbaiting – other than scattering out a few hook bait fragments – is not required. Indeed, it might have the reverse effect and actually scare off a handful of wily old tench from approaching the swim. On the other hand, where tench are present in abundant numbers and need to be weaned away from their daily diet of aquatic insects, shrimps, bloodworms and the like, a liberal helping of groundbait, incorporating hook-bait fragments, is very much the order of the day.

For the groundbait base there is nothing to beat plain brown breadcrumbs. If it is going to be packed into an open-ended feeder, the crumbs need to be coarse so that they create an exploding effect when they suddenly swell on absorbing water. If the groundbait is going to be thrown or catapulted, the crumbs can be coarse or fine.

To the plain crumb, add a few cupfuls each of maize meal (to give that 'sweetcorn' appeal), salmon fry crumbs or ground trout pellets, hempseed or boiled rice, plus fragments of the hook-bait such as casters, maggots, chopped worms, sweetcorn or chopped mini boilies. A spoonful or two (per bucket) of yellow or orange powder dye helps to cloud water which is on the clear side.

I have been known to mix this up two or three days prior to using it, to give the natural yeasts time to start fermenting. Tench adore the smell, but you would be well advised not to squeeze out the balls ready for throwing in the early morning if you have a hangover.

PRE-BAITING, DRAGGING AND RAKING

Whenever time permits I like to pre-bait new areas or new fisheries at least a night or two before the first early-morning fishing session. If tench in good numbers are known to be there, then half a bucket of groundbait is a

Swims that are completely choked with surface plants such as the dwarf pond lily and therefore unfishable can, with the help of a weed rake or drag, quickly be transformed into ideal float-fishing spots.

good measure to start with. More can always be introduced during the session if the tench continue to feed well into daylight following the magical dawn-feeding period. A small quantity of fresh blood (obtainable from a butcher) mixed into the groundbait provides added attraction for the fish, especially after the swim has been raked or dragged.

Opinions vary as to when is the best time to drag a tench swim; or if to drag it at all. Some say the evening is best before a dawn start, some say immediately prior to fishing. Having taken good hauls after dragging at both times, I am not really fussy. However, I would perhaps bend towards the latter view on the grounds that I won't have missed any tench attracted to the area during the night which have subsequently departed, bellies full of free feed.

It is necessary to understand what is achieved by raking out a clear patch of water amongst dense weed, apart from allowing the fish to move about more freely, because the effect can prove three-fold.

Firstly, the sound waves attract tench (the most curious of fishes) to the area like bees to a honey-pot. Secondly, they have a nice surprise when they arrive because all the tiny, single items of food which they normally have to grub about to find are conveniently presented – along with your loose feed. Lastly, the thick cloud of silt which might be held in suspension for up to several hours depending upon water temperature and the number of tench which arrive in the swim and keep it churned up, makes them feel more secure.

If you own a pair of chest-waders, and your favourite tench lake is neither too deep nor too silty, take along a long-handled garden rake and give the bottom, whether weedy or not, a good raking. I wish I had a fiver for every time during high summer that I have stripped down to my underpants and got in to clear a swim of its weeds, or simply to churn the bottom up. Neighbouring anglers might hand out a few old-fashioned looks, but their faces soon change when they see your rod bending a few minutes later. And don't be afraid to get out there and give the bottom a good going over at any time of the day, especially when the sun is well up, sport has stopped and the tench have retreated into the thickest weed. It cannot do anything but improve your chances.

CHAPTER SIX

TECHNIQUES AND RIGS

FREELINING

Freelining is exactly what the term implies: nothing is attached to the line that could impair natural presentation, only the hook and bait. The line is free of all shots, floats and ledger rigs. This is why the technique produces such confident bites from tench in clear waters which, through suspicion, might otherwise dither or play about with the bait, especially float-fished baits where the line is vertical from shots to float as in the lift method.

Large baits heavy enough in themselves to disguise the hook and neutralize its weight, such as the insides of a whole swan mussel, a lump of trout pellet paste or a lobworm, are each also heavy enough to cast accurately from a well-filled spool without added weight. Freelining is therefore a method which can only be practised at close range where tench are attracted to natural habitats: gaps between beds of marginal sedges, rushes or reeds; alongside and even into beds of lily pads; beneath the overhanging branches of willow or alder; and beside trees whose lower limbs are part sunken.

Some of the most exciting tench I have caught while freelining came during the heat of the afternoon from beneath a canopy of partly submerged rhododendrons. These particular tench live in a beautiful, secluded mere and invariably disappeared from all the popular swims once the sun rose high in the sky. Even from my spying tree, an old cedar whose branches reached out a good 30 ft above the surface, I could see nothing through the crystal-clear water, which was nowhere deeper than 4 ft, save for shoals of immature rudd and countless mussel shells. It was so clear that even those spots where the resident heron liked to fish could be pinpointed by the preponderance of open mussel shells close in to the bank.

It was a phenomenon which always had me puzzled until one afternoon when, completely by accident, whilst peering into the water through polaroid glasses I happened to notice a pair of black tails protruding from beneath the maze of partly-sunken rhododendron branches hanging way out over the margins.

Despite a depth of just 18 in, there were days when it seemed as though the mere's entire population of tench would take refuge in the shade of just two albeit large rhododendrons. The attraction was two-fold: subdued light in a mere barren of lilies, combined with a readily available food source of aquatic insect larvae clinging to the sunken woodwork.

I would flip a fat lobworm hooked once only through the head by a size 6 hook, tied direct to 6 lb line (the beauty of freelining is that it permits the use of sensible tackle), into the gaps between the branches and allow it to reach bottom. If there was no response after a minute or so I twitched it back slowly, pausing every so often in case it had been sighted.

A slamming take more reminiscent of weed-raft chub than tench could happen at any moment. A large lump of

Opposite: Using the tall stems of yellow iris as cover, John kneels low to freeline a whole lobworm to tench working the warm marginal shallows.

A bunch of maggots, fished tight up to a bed of sweet reed grass beneath a waggler in just 3 ft of water, accounted for this plump 5 lb gravel-pit tench.

breadflake was always a good substitute when the lobworms ran out, or were unobtainable, and the meaty
insides of a swan mussel also produced results. Unfortunately, a higher ratio of eels to tench than was desirable
invariably came to mussel, so the gyrating lobworm was
always favourite.

Anglers who have only ever float-fished for tench, using
light float tackle in heavily fished waters and straining their
eyes for those tiny dips or lifts of the float tip in order to
strike, would not believe the way in which tench run off
with a freelined bait. But then, with an unweighted bait
they have no reason to be fussy. They simply suck it in and
move off looking for the next meal, lifting the line in a
glorious, unmissable, almost carp-like run.

If immediate bites are expected, do not bother with
indicators. Hold the rod and keep your eyes glued to the
bow in the line from rod tip to surface. If not, hang a
lightweight foil indicator on a 2 ft drop between butt ring
and reel, after positioning the rod on two rests with the tip
pointing directly at the bait. Whack the hook home just
before the indicator slams against the butt ring.

With minimal resistance on the line, the tench is just as
likely to swim towards the rod and give a 'drop back',
whereupon the indicator suddenly falls to the ground. This
is a good reason for always keeping the bale arm closed
when freelining, enabling you to go straight into a 'wind-
cum-strike' routine in order to pick up the line and punch
the hook home.

When freelining into darkness or when tench activity is
on the slow side, rig up an electric alarm in conjunction
with the foil indicator so you can relax. You can certainly
afford to, because bites are nearly always positive.

FLOAT FISHING

The lift method

No other float-fishing technique has been so exhaustively
described as the famous lift method. Yet even now,
almost 40 years since the Taylor brothers first popularized
the method back in the 1950s with their huge catches of

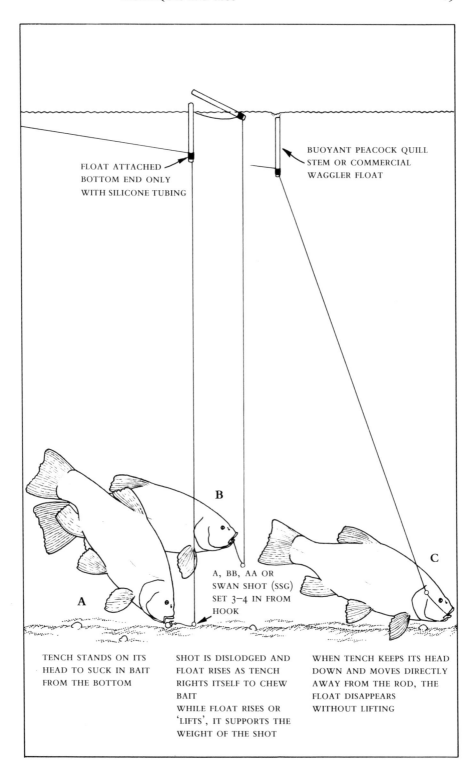

FLOAT ATTACHED
BOTTOM END ONLY
WITH SILICONE TUBING

BUOYANT PEACOCK QUILL
STEM OR COMMERCIAL
WAGGLER FLOAT

B

A, BB, AA OR
SWAN SHOT (SSG)
SET 3–4 IN FROM
HOOK

A

C

TENCH STANDS ON ITS
HEAD TO SUCK IN BAIT
FROM THE BOTTOM

SHOT IS DISLODGED AND
FLOAT RISES AS TENCH
RIGHTS ITSELF TO CHEW
BAIT
WHILE FLOAT RISES OR
'LIFTS', IT SUPPORTS THE
WEIGHT OF THE SHOT

WHEN TENCH KEEPS ITS HEAD
DOWN AND MOVES DIRECTLY
AWAY FROM THE ROD, THE
FLOAT DISAPPEARS
WITHOUT LIFTING

When numbers of tench are feeding in earnest and sending streams of bubbles up to the surface, the most effective method of presentation is to float-fish using the lift rig, and instantly hit any positive movement.

tench from the lakes at Wooton Underwood, the vast majority of anglers still get it wrong because they fail to grasp the basic principle of the lift. Once and for all let me explain how this great technique actually works.

The lift is particularly successful with, and suited to, the tench as a species because of the way in which they stand on their heads to suck in bottom-fished baits (see 'Feeding'). They are obliged to perform a headstand because their mouth is upturned. So when they decide that here on the bottom is a particle of food they fancy eating (your bait) they tilt their head down and suck it up. All being well they then return to an even keel while chewing the food. I have already mentioned that tench are equipped with powerful pharnygeal teeth to split a worm into pulp or crush the juices from maggots and casters. They then spit out the hook because it is indigestible – not necessarily as is often assumed, because it is something to be scared of – just as they do other unwanted items such as twigs, leaves, empty caddis cases, bits of weed, which get taken up as they vacuum the bottom. This is why an angler whose lift rig is incorrectly shotted (the shot being too far away from the hook) will reel in time and time again with empty maggot skins on the hook, without seeing the slightest indication of a bite.

The essence of fishing the lift is to set the float (a length of peacock quill or commercial waggler) a little overdepth,

attached bottom end only with a piece of silicone tubing and *not* locking shots. I'll say that again: *not* locking shots. You do not want any shots anywhere near the float. All the shot loading, a BB, an AA, or a single swan shot (depending on casting requirements) must be fixed just 3–4 in from the hook (see fig. 12A). When the tench sucks up the bait and rights itself, thus dislodging the shot, the float starts to 'lift' (hence the method's name) and may even fall flat. But more importantly: while it is 'lifting' it is helping to support the weight of the shot. Of course, once the float lays completely flat (fig. 12B) the tench is fully supporting the weight of that shot and could eject the bait. This is why you should always strike as the float 'lifts'.

Some anglers suffer a mental block at this stage; because the float is still visible they do not consider the bite worth striking. If you leave the bite to develop further, the float may cock again and slowly slide beneath the surface in one of those classic 'Mr Crabtree' tench bites as the tench moves along the bottom directly away from the rod. However, this seldom happens. And you cannot risk waiting for such a positive indication because the tench will probably drop the bait.

This tench fisherman knows all about maximizing on bites when presenting the lift rig. He is holding the rod in a comfortable, relaxed, yet expectant manner, and is ready to strike quickly into the tiniest movement of the float tip.

If, however, from the moment it sucks up the bait the tench keeps its head down and carries on going directly away from the rod, the float without any pre-warning whatsoever (occasionally it might 'bob' first) will simply disappear as in fig. 12C. And this is the beauty behind the lift method – it allows you to interpret exactly what is happening down below.

When bites are expected at regular intervals you will convert considerably more (even the tiniest lifts and dips) into tench in the net if you hold the rod throughout. It may only take a split second to reach down and grab the rod set in rests, but the tench can blow the bait out even quicker. Besides, striking immediately allows you to bend the rod into a full curve and apply sufficient pressure against a tench hooked beside potential snags and to get it well under control before it can retaliate.

There is another advantage in holding the rod when fishing the lift. By gently moving the bait along the bottom you can encourage difficult tench to make a quick decision and grab the bait. This works especially well when the bait is presented over a clean bottom – either silt, mud or gravel – because as you slowly give the reel handle half a turn (providing the line is tight from float to rod tip) the inherent buoyancy of peacock quill will help the shot move along the bottom. Initially it will go under as you start to wind but will pop up again a second or two later. In the meantime, a tench may be aroused by the bait's sudden audacity in moving away, and make a sudden grab for it, resulting in a very quick 'lift' or 'dip'. If you are holding the rod you can strike these bites instantly, producing tench which would otherwise not be caught.

Tench can invariably be induced into feeding by bait movement, especially with baits which move anyway like maggots and worms. It is a characteristic trait which we all experience from time to time, the classic example being the ledger indicator which is yanked from your grasp (see 'Ledgering', p. 113) as you try desperately to reset it, having just moved the bait anything from a few inches to a couple of feet. And there is no better way of moving the bait while remaining ready to deal with an instant bite than presenting the lift rig.

For 'twitching' the bait over an uneven bottom, use a longer (and thus more buoyant) peacock quill than the shot

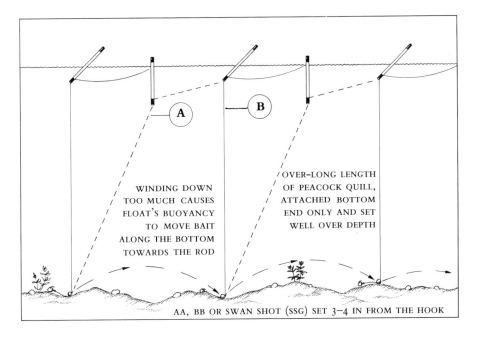

WINDING DOWN
TOO MUCH CAUSES
FLOAT'S BUOYANCY
TO MOVE BAIT
ALONG THE BOTTOM
TOWARDS THE ROD

OVER-LONG LENGTH
OF PEACOCK QUILL,
ATTACHED BOTTOM
END ONLY AND SET
WELL OVER DEPTH

AA, BB OR SWAN SHOT (SSG) SET 3–4 IN FROM THE HOOK

requires. For example, if it is set shallower than the swim depth, the float should cock but with a good 2 in above the surface. Then reset it so that it is slightly over-depth and cast out, gently tightening up until only 1 in of the tip is visible (fig. 13A). You will know the set-up is correct when you wind down too much and the float lifts the shot along the bottom and keels over (fig. 13B). Just tighten up again, as this is exactly what it is supposed to do.

FIGURE 13 *Using the lift rig to twitch the bait along an uneven bottom*

The lift can be used effectively with most baits (except large mouthfuls), and sometimes it pays to juggle about with the shot, moving it a little closer to the hook or a little further away than the recommended 3–4 in. When tench are especially shy in clear water conditions, I use a single BB (it is almost impossible to fish the lift effectively with a smaller shot) pinched on just 2 in from the hook and select a short, super-slim length of quill. Then I wind down until the top of the quill is a mere blimp in the surface film, and subsequently strike at the slightest movement up or down.

This super-sensitive rig is great for bugging the 'bubblers', tench which are rooting just beyond the marginal lilies quite close in, where the bubbles of individual fish can be identified. Make a calculated guess as to which direction the tench is heading and cast a little to the right or left of where bubbles last erupted. Be

There is nothing quite so nice as catching tench close in on light float tackle and a centre-pin reel.

FIGURE 14
(Opposite) *Bodied
waggler or driftbeater
rig*

impatient for bites, and keep casting to rising bubbles until
an instant bite occurs. It is a fascinating and active way of
taking tench.

Because an upward strike is imperative with the lift
method to pick up the slack created by the tench lifting the
bait and shot, it can only be used as a close-range
technique. If you want to float-fish for tench which are
actively feeding considerably further than say a couple of
rod lengths out, particularly in windy weather, the line
must be sunk or the float will drag under. This means you
cannot strike upwards, or continue to use quite the same
rig, so no longer can just a single shot be used.

Bodied waggler or driftbeater rig

To reach greater distances, you require a float taking a fair
shotting capacity – anywhere from 3AA to 2½ swan shot –
and this means using a bodied waggler or a driftbeater.
The float is locked by a BB on both sides, with the bulk
shot set at mid depth, leaving a small shot (no. 1 or no. 3)
to go near the hook, and a BB between it and the bulk shot
(fig. 14).

To facilitate a quick change of float as surface conditions
alter, use a swivel float attachment into which the float can
instantly be pushed or removed. Lift bites on this rig are
obviously not going to make the float come flying out of
the water. However, with the bottom shot close to the
hook, if the float is 'lifted' the float top will rise the same
distance as it is sunk by that shot. So, after casting and
winding the rig back over the swim with the rod tip
beneath the surface to sink the line, memorize the level of
the float in the water when the tip eventually settles once
the BB shot is 'hanging', and then by how much further it
sinks when the bottom shot hangs the bait just on the
bottom.

In all probability most bites on this float rig will consist
of a slow disappearance of the tip; you reply with a strong
scything, sideways strike, keeping the rod tip low to the
water to pick up maximum line and put the hook home.
Gentle lift bites will occur, however, so watch carefully for
the tip rising and always remember to strike sideways.

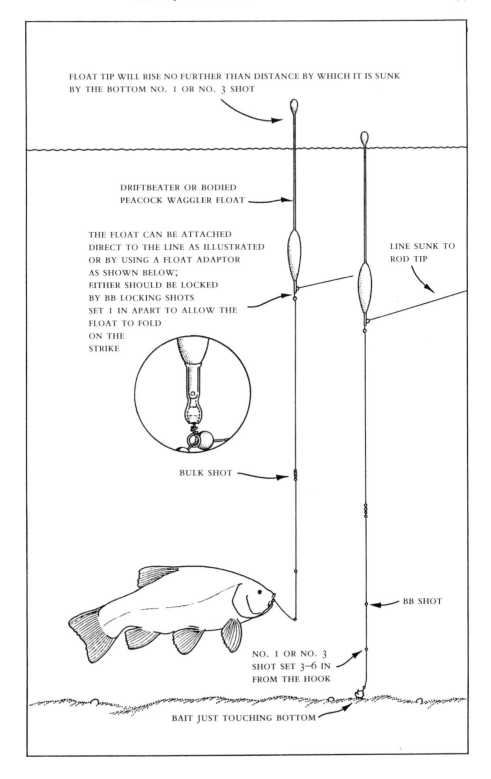

FLOAT TIP WILL RISE NO FURTHER THAN DISTANCE BY WHICH IT IS SUNK
BY THE BOTTOM NO. 1 OR NO. 3 SHOT

DRIFTBEATER OR BODIED
PEACOCK WAGGLER FLOAT

LINE SUNK TO
ROD TIP

THE FLOAT CAN BE ATTACHED
DIRECT TO THE LINE AS ILLUSTRATED
OR BY USING A FLOAT ADAPTOR
AS SHOWN BELOW;
EITHER SHOULD BE LOCKED
BY BB LOCKING SHOTS
SET 1 IN APART TO ALLOW THE
FLOAT TO FOLD
ON THE
STRIKE

BULK SHOT

BB SHOT

NO. 1 OR NO. 3
SHOT SET 3–6 IN
FROM THE HOOK

BAIT JUST TOUCHING BOTTOM

I like a long, thickish, straight peacock waggler for float ledgering, and attach it to the line with a ⅜ in length of silicone tubing around the bottom stem.

The zoomer rig

This is a deadly float rig for placing the bait close up to reed-lines or against lily-beds in clear water conditions, where bites materialize only if the bait is presented in the tench's habitat (fig. 16A). Simply rig up an onion or zoomer with the bulk shot at the base of the float. After plummeting the depth accurately, pinch on a BB shot around 5 in from the hook, so it comes to rest just on the bottom. Then, because the float precedes the hook and shot, you can allow it almost to bump against the reed-line before stopping the cast, knowing the bait will angle back down through the water to settle mere inches away from the leading reeds, in full view of patrolling tench.

This method also pays dividends on even-depth, clear-watered lakes and meres where dinghies or punts are used (fig. 16B). If beds of marginal reeds, rushes or sedges are the only cover, that is where the tench will be. Row up quietly to within practical casting distance and position the boat side-on to the reed-line. Anchor it by slipping a mud-weight over the side at each end.

As the float cannot be wound back with the rod tip held beneath the surface to sink the line (which would only bring the bait away from the reeds), take along a small (medicine) bottle of neat washing-up liquid and dab a finger-full over the spool every so often. The line will then sink willingly and instantly, after which you can very gently tighten up without pulling the float away from the reeds. Hold the rod whenever bites are expected.

Keep catapulting fragments of loose feed like sweetcorn, maggots, casters or worms along the reed-line for a distance of several yards either side of the float, and tench might be encouraged to work the area all day long.

As a last resort when bites appear to have finally dried up once the sun rises high in the sky, try this favourite old all-or-nothing ruse. Row over to reeds and with an oar spend 15 minutes clouding up the bottom silt. Then return to your anchorage and commence fishing.

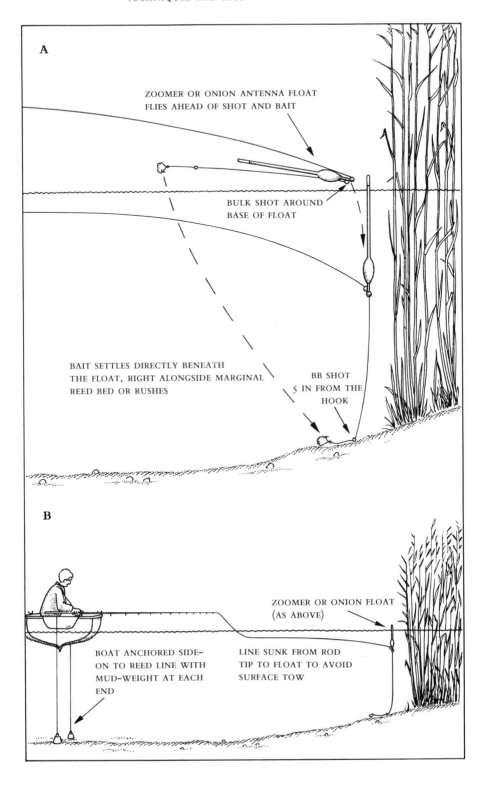

A

ZOOMER OR ONION ANTENNA FLOAT
FLIES AHEAD OF SHOT AND BAIT

BULK SHOT AROUND
BASE OF FLOAT

BAIT SETTLES DIRECTLY BENEATH
THE FLOAT, RIGHT ALONGSIDE MARGINAL
REED BED OR RUSHES

BB SHOT
5 IN FROM THE
HOOK

B

ZOOMER OR ONION FLOAT
(AS ABOVE)

BOAT ANCHORED SIDE-
ON TO REED LINE WITH
MUD-WEIGHT AT EACH
END

LINE SUNK FROM ROD
TIP TO FLOAT TO AVOID
SURFACE TOW

Anchoring the boat quietly away from the reed beds, and casting a zoomer float rig close up alongside the stems, puts the bait exactly where tench feed naturally.

The flat peacock rig

When tackling dense reed-lines along your own bank, either from wooden staging or from marshy ground, it is a waste of time to cast out over the reeds and expect tench to feed in open water, unless the water is well coloured. They are much more likely to be mere feet away, working through the reeds or rushes (see 'Feeding').

Such swims demand a stealthy approach (fig. 17). You need to sit or kneel a few feet back from the water-line with a bait hanging right beneath the rod tip just 2 to 3 yd out, where tench will be feeding between the stems. The type of float is not really important at such close range. A tiny waggler, or even 2 in of slim unpainted peacock quill, will suffice. In the absence of wind or surface tow, I like the quill fixed top and bottom to present it lying 'flat' on the surface.

The beauty of the 'flat' float is that unbelievably confident bites will result. The quill slides along the surface, following the direction of the tench, and disappears with the same confidence fish show to freelined offerings. Only one small shot is attached, around 12 in from the bait. It does not matter what size shot you use, because it doesn't cock the float. If you are fishing right in amongst marginal stems pre-baiting is not really necessary because the tench are already there. More often than not, groups of

As far as the hungry tench is concerned, this weedy corner of the lake is ideal. Free-lining, or use of the flat peacock float rig with the hook tied direct to a 6 lb reel line and baits like a whole lobworm or luncheon meat cube, are recommended tactics.

stems can be seen swaying as fish root between them. However, you will need to creep about to catch them at such close quarters. Just scatter a handful of bait fragments among the stems (pieces of flake or broken worms) to keep fish in the area, and to encourage them to return each time one is caught and they temporarily disappear.

FIGURE 17 *Flat peacock rig. The peacock quill is fixed top and bottom. The hook bait can be bread flake, lobworm, etc.*

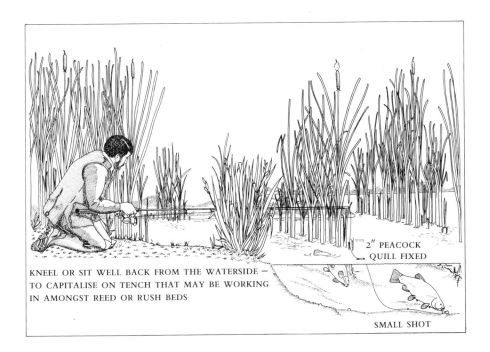

2″ PEACOCK QUILL FIXED

KNEEL OR SIT WELL BACK FROM THE WATERSIDE – TO CAPITALISE ON TENCH THAT MAY BE WORKING IN AMONGST REED OR RUSH BEDS

SMALL SHOT

Though the float may be light, this is certainly not a
light-tackle method. You will need all of a 6 lb test line to
subdue even modest-sized tench of 2–3 lb in exciting hit
and haul tussles.

FLOAT FISHING AT NIGHT

Without question, and especially where the water is gin-
clear for most of the summer, fishing for tench from dusk
into darkness, perhaps even all night through, offers the
best chance of success. I know several lakes, meres and pits
where, for the last two hours of daylight, you need to scale
down almost to match tackle to encourage even an
occasional, tentative bite. As soon as the light starts to go,
however, and it becomes difficult for the human eye to
distinguish the bottom through just 2 to 3 ft of clear water,
the tench lose their natural caution and start to bite
positively. And this phenomenon is not applicable only to
hard-fished, public tench fisheries.

So if bites are hard to come by wherever you fish during
the daytime, try a spot of night fishing. It can be magical,
provided you choose a suitable night on your first attempt.
Tench are not likely to be receptive to your bait, for
instance, during a howling gale accompanied by torrential
rain and a sudden drop in temperature.

If you prefer the simplicity of float fishing and there is a
reasonable depth along the margins where tench can be
encouraged to feed with a little pre-baiting, the good old
lift method is the rig to use (p. 88). Follow exactly my
advice for presenting the lift, and fix a luminous element to
the top of the float.

Whether your session turns into an all-nighter, or lasts
for just a few hours, you want to avoid eye strain, and the
most pleasant of luminous elements to watch continuously
are the chemical 'starlights', which come in a choice of
three sizes. These consist of a clear plastic tube containing
two chemicals which, once you bend the tube and shake it,
mix together and become luminous for about eight hours.
I prefer the mini 'starlights', which come two to a packet
complete with a length of clear tubing. If you are using a
thin stem of peacock quill, the tubing supplied fits snuggly

over the tip with the starlight slotting into the other end.

Both the Drennan polywag and onion floats (which both work well fished lift style), of any shotting capacity, also have tips of the right diameter. Alternatively, purchase the Drennan clear-bodied, insert-crystal wagglers, which have detachable tips into which the Drennan 'night light' can be fitted. These are available in three sizes, large (for distance fishing), standard and minis, the last two being quite sufficient and easily seen just like the 'starlights', up to three rod lengths out.

As bites at night tend to be far more positive than those experienced in the daytime, resist the temptation to wind the float tip down so only the merest tip is visible, or you will be forever striking at ghosts. By all means hold the rod to capitalize on bites when they are occurring frequently, but when times are slow, try to relax by positioning the rod close to hand, supported horizontally on two rests.

Wherever there is a slight draw on the surface, the float might be slowly dragged under. Simply push the back rod rest down a little to angle the tip of the rod upwards, thus lifting sufficient line off the surface for the float tip to reappear. You will gradually learn these little tricks. You will also quickly discover to switch on a torch *only* when it is absolutely necessary (such as when the line is tangled) because night vision is instantly ruined by torchlight. It takes several minutes before your eyes can readjust to the dark again, making items such as the bait and your landing-net visible once more.

LEDGERING

Although there are dozens of different float rigs for catching tench (and everyone has his favourites), the selection just described should prove more than adequate wherever and whenever you fish. There will, however, be many occasions throughout the summer months when the pleasure of watching a float must reluctantly be replaced by the effectiveness of the ledger (and particularly of feeder fishing) if you wish to catch tench from a wide spectrum of waters.

Float fishing for tench at night is now a formality thanks to these extra-bright, luminous 'starlight' elements. They push on to any float tip via a sleeve of silicone tubing.

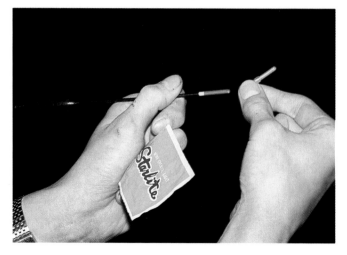

Tench inhabiting distant troughs and gullies situated, say, 40 yd or more out from the bank in huge gravel pit complexes can only be tackled effectively by ledgering. Large, clear-watered estate lakes where the tench always seem to keep well out because the marginal water is so shallow, or because there is a complete absence of soft weed, again demand ledgering tactics. So too do waters with hard bottoms, such as brick-laid reservoirs and deep, newly dug gravel or clay pits, where weed beds or layers of silt have yet to accumulate, and where subsequently the tench may never be seen bubbling enough to pinpoint them with float tackle. Ledgering at least gives you the option of searching for them 'grid style' until bites materialize.

In fact, most large sheets of water are far more effectively fished with ledgering techniques because of weather conditions alone. To cast accurately and control a float over long distances in the windy conditions which invariably prevail on open sheets of water is an impossible task. And on the calmest day, there might well be a draw or pull on the surface to irritate the most ardent of float-fishermen.

Fixed paternoster

The fixed paternoster is a simple follow-on from freelining (p. 85), and is used to reach fish beyond the casting range

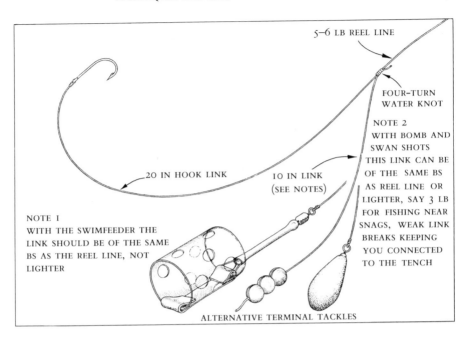

5–6 LB REEL LINE

FOUR–TURN WATER KNOT

NOTE 2 WITH BOMB AND SWAN SHOTS THIS LINK CAN BE OF THE SAME BS AS REEL LINE OR LIGHTER, SAY 3 LB FOR FISHING NEAR SNAGS, WEAK LINK BREAKS KEEPING YOU CONNECTED TO THE TENCH

20 IN HOOK LINK

10 IN LINK (SEE NOTES)

NOTE I WITH THE SWIMFEEDER THE LINK SHOULD BE OF THE SAME BS AS THE REEL LINE, NOT LIGHTER

ALTERNATIVE TERMINAL TACKLES

of weightless tackle. It is formed by adding a simple fixed-bomb paternoster to the reel line 20 in above the hook (fig. 18). The fixed-bomb paternoster comprises a 10 in link (of reel line), tied in using a four-turn water knot (p. 53), to which a bomb or a string of swan shots is added. Because their weight is distributed over a greater surface area, a string of swan shots (unlike a dense bomb), does not drop down through thick weed. Instead, the swan shot usually rest on top. And provided they have been pinched on lightly, they will slide off easily even if they become snagged. Conversely, if snags are expected, use a lighter test for the link, say 3 lb, which should break and ditch the swan shots or bomb, leaving you free to play the tench. Incidentally, I rarely use less than a 5 lb test reel line when ledgering for tench; more often than not I put my faith in 6 lb test, which copes with the rigours of continuous casting and being dragged across weed-beds, over shallow bars and even along the bottom. You can use lighter hook lengths, but there is no point in going lighter on the reel line. To present a buoyant bait, like an air injected lob, bread crust or a pop-up boilie, several inches above dense bottom weed simply add a swan shot or two a few inches above the hook (fig. 19).

This simple ledger rig will suffice for a whole variety of

FIGURE 18 *Fixed paternoster ledger*

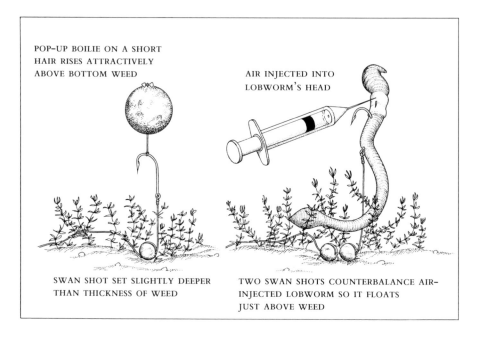

POP-UP BOILIE ON A SHORT
HAIR RISES ATTRACTIVELY
ABOVE BOTTOM WEED

AIR INJECTED INTO
LOBWORM'S HEAD

SWAN SHOT SET SLIGHTLY DEEPER
THAN THICKNESS OF WEED

TWO SWAN SHOTS COUNTERBALANCE AIR-
INJECTED LOBWORM SO IT FLOATS
JUST ABOVE WEED

FIGURE 19 *Presenting buoyant baits over dense bottom weed*

baits in addition to boilies and worms, including meat cubes, sweetcorn, maggots, soft pastes and bread flake, presented wherever loose feed or groundbait has been either catapulted or thrown in. Beyond this range you simply exchange the bomb or swan shots for a swimfeeder – to be more precise, an open-ended swimfeeder.

Feeder fishing

If conditions require a slow dispersal of, say, maggots, such as when ledgering for tench during the winter in very mild spells (see 'Winter tench', pp. 41–3), a block-end feeder such as the Drennan 'feeder link' fits the bill perfectly. However, in summer this is not the case. Then I want the feeder to explode its load just before, or as, it hits bottom, thus creating an instant food source for the tench to home in on. The best open-ended feeders are the plain, plastic, clear or green open-ends with a lead strip at the base, or the self-weighted cage feeders. Both permit the instant bait dispersal of breadcrumb groundbait, provided that the crumbs are not over-wetted. Coarse, slightly dampened crumb is preferable, because it really does explode once the crumbs expand on impact with the water.

For putting out just groundbait, I use both cage and plastic open-ended feeders. If I want a crumb plug at each end, with a filling of hook bait samples like corn, maggots or casters, the open-ended feeder is best. Incidentally, to stop feeder maggots from burrowing into soft silt and disappearing (something they can do with surprising speed) immerse them for just a couple of seconds in boiling water and dry off with maize meal or bread crumbs. They will look a little 'stretched' when killed in this manner, but tench gobble them up just the same and I cannot remember suffering any lack of bites when using them on the hook.

Do not worry about the heavy splash made by a feeder when it hits the water, because the tench come to associate it with the arrival of free food. The secret is to keep casting the feeder out every 10 minutes or so, whether tench respond or not. In this way, small piles of bait are deposited over a fairly tight area, ready for the moment when they move in to inspect it. And they will – just have faith in their inquisitiveness.

In effect, you create (often in a ridiculously short space of time) your own tench swim, with fish eventually moving about on the bottom from one pile of bait to another. Casting needs to be accurate so that you do not spread bait, and therefore tench, over too wide an area.

A two-rod set-up is beneficial when feeder-fishing. Double the bait is deposited, and you have the option at will to use one of the rods as the 'locator' when you think the tench may have moved position, keeping the other over the original baited area.

Striking

The ideal tool for ledgering, with or without feeders, is a 1¼ lb text curve, 11 ft or 12 ft carbon Avon rod (see p. 46–8). I prefer the 12-footer for optimum line pick up when long-range fishing. After casting out, each rod is pointed at the bait to minimize resistance from biting fish and to maximize striking efficiency. Remember that in really shallow water a low, sideways strike will pick up more line because it pulls it through the water as opposed to lifting it upwards against the surface tension (fig. 20A). On the other hand, when presenting the bait into deep-

Ledgering into deep gullies way out from the margins in really clear-watered gravel pits is the most effective way of catching tench right through the day. A reduction in both hook-length strength and hook sizes is imperative for inducing bites in bright conditions.

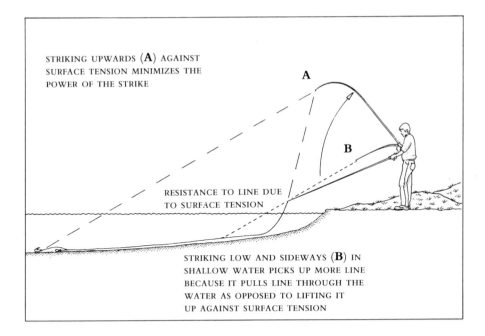

STRIKING UPWARDS (**A**) AGAINST
SURFACE TENSION MINIMIZES THE
POWER OF THE STRIKE

A

B

RESISTANCE TO LINE DUE
TO SURFACE TENSION

STRIKING LOW AND SIDEWAYS (**B**) IN
SHALLOW WATER PICKS UP MORE LINE
BECAUSE IT PULLS LINE THROUGH THE
WATER AS OPPOSED TO LIFTING IT
UP AGAINST SURFACE TENSION

FIGURE 20A
Striking in
shallow water

water swims, an upwards strike is more advantageous
(fig. 20B).

Try to tighten up gently after casting, to sink the line
fully, so that it settles in a straight line between feeder and
rod tip, not in a huge belly. Then clip on the indicator (see
pp. 55–60). A little washing-up liquid dabbed around the
line on the spool will help it sink quickly, so keep a bottle
handy. In strong winds, endeavour to fish directly into the
wind. Otherwise, pinch a swan shot or two on to the
bobbin line to stop any underwater tow bellying the line
between feeder and rod tip, thus reducing the effectiveness
of the strike. Remember that if the line is not reasonably
tight from feeder to rod, setting the hook becomes more of
a problem the further out you fish. This may occur when
you are fishing over dense beds of soft weed if the rods are
set too low to the surface. Bite indication will be hampered
if the line actually rests on the weed, resulting in a much
reduced movement of the bobbin. The remedy here is to
set the rods as high as you can, keeping as much line as
possible off the weed and keeping it relatively tight from
tip to feeder. Unfortunately this becomes difficult in
strong winds because extra line above the surface creates
additional wind resistance. The only recourse is to add still
more swan shots to the bobbin retaining-cord.

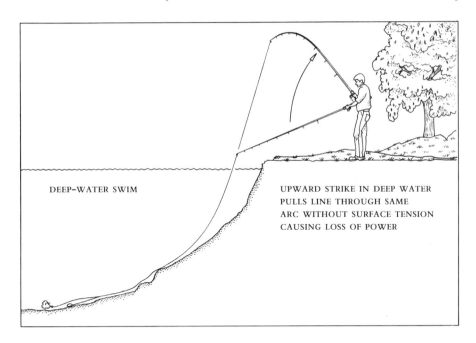

DEEP-WATER SWIM

UPWARD STRIKE IN DEEP WATER
PULLS LINE THROUGH SAME
ARC WITHOUT SURFACE TENSION
CAUSING LOSS OF POWER

Bite indication

FIGURE 20B
Striking in
deep water

During the initial hours of feeder-fishing in a 'new' swim, bites will invariably consist of really positive lifts of the bobbin, with the Optonic screeching out several bleeps before the bobbin clangs against the butt ring. In this situation, allow a drop of around 18 in. The choice of combining the bobbin with an electric alarm as the front rod rest is, of course, optional. I would suggest, however, that where long all-day or all-night sessions are concerned, the excessive concentration demanded by staring continually at the bobbins, not daring to look away in case one moves (and that is when they always do move) is reason enough to use the combination. In addition, the alarm/bobbin set up is by far the most efficient for all feeder-fishing for tench. I find that it allows a very relaxed approach to fishing, giving me time to study wildlife through the binoculars and to scan the surface for bubbles. Yet I am ready to strike instantly the very second the alarm issues its warning bleeps.

Bonus fish can often be caught as a result of studying surface activity in between bites. Tench caught well away from the main feeding area often result from quickly

John dares the bobbin to move and stands poised for a long sweeping strike when distance fishing the feeder for tench in a shallow, Norfolk estate lake. Twitcher-hitting at its best.

reeling in one of the baits and repositioning it close to any
sudden eruption of bubbles, or to a porpoising fish.

The twitching cycle

As the tench become more preoccupied with loose feed
deposited by the feeder, and as your casting becomes more
accurate, concentrating good numbers of tench into a
comparatively confined area, tiny twitch bites – 1 to 2 in
lifts or drops of the bobbin – will become commonplace.

Now is the time to reduce both the bobbin drop so that
small movements are more noticeable, and the hook length
to just 6 in enabling you to see bites much earlier. Keep the
10 in feeder link (fig. 21). Quite simply the tench are no
longer moving away with the bait to another patch of
food, they are consuming it on the spot. Bites which
merely lift or drop back the bobbin by ¼ in may seem to
be the work of small fish instead of tench, but that is
because they have become so preoccupied and so confident,
with an excess of food spread around them, that they have
little reason to move.

If on a standard hook tail (18–20 in long) you repeatedly
reel in sucked maggots or sweetcorn skins, or your worms
have had all the goodness crushed out of them, the bait
must have been sucked back to the pharnygeal teeth,
chewed for a while, and then spat out. It is wise to strike
promptly at the slightest twitch or jingle of the bobbin
once the twitching cycle begins – once you have shortened
the hook length.

On calm days you can forget the bobbin altogether after
tightening up, and simply watch the line itself where it
enters the water, hitting the slightest lift or drop back no
matter how seemingly insignificant.

If bites still prove conspicuous by their absence, and you
believe tench are still in the swim – as may be the case in
the middle of the day when parts of the terminal rig look
far more obvious in very clear water – it is time to reduce
the hook length from 6, 5 or 4 lb to just 3 lb, and to step
down in hook size, presenting smaller baits. While a
number 10 hook holding four grains of corn or five
maggots may be the taking formula at 6 am, by 11.30 am,
when the sun is high above the water, those same tench

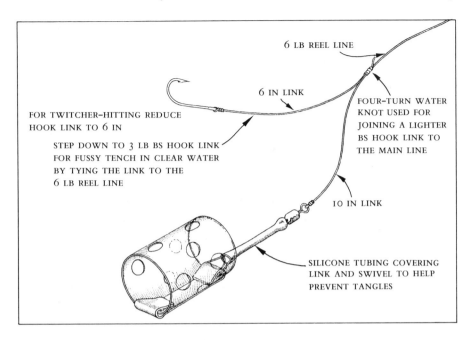

6 LB REEL LINE

6 IN LINK

FOUR-TURN WATER
KNOT USED FOR
JOINING A LIGHTER
BS HOOK LINK TO
THE MAIN LINE

FOR TWITCHER-HITTING REDUCE
HOOK LINK TO 6 IN

STEP DOWN TO 3 LB BS HOOK LINK
FOR FUSSY TENCH IN CLEAR WATER
BY TYING THE LINK TO THE
6 LB REEL LINE

10 IN LINK

SILICONE TUBING COVERING
LINK AND SWIVEL TO HELP
PREVENT TANGLES

FIGURE 21
'Twitcher-hitting'

may not provide you with a hittable bite until you offer them a size 16 holding two casters. When bites are not forthcoming, it is worth trying anything. However, don't be tempted to go down to a lighter hook length than the tench can be safely extracted with. Consider the weed growth, snags, and the general size of the fish expected and only step down accordingly.

I like to try to stimulate bites by constantly changing hook baits (regardless of what has been fed in), from maggots to corn, flake to worms and back again. Occasionally a buoyant bait presented on the drop will bring immediate action simply because it's different. Or try offerings like casters and crust cocktails, casters and corn, flake and maggots, and so on. Never be afraid to experiment. Try twitching the bait in, pausing for 30 seconds or so between each half or full slow crank of the handle. This of course is suicidal in thick weed, but where the bottom is reasonably clean it is a deadly technique which often leaves you next to no time between twitches to reset the bobbin before it is yanked upwards.

As you might a float, try and relate movements of the bobbin to what is actually happening at the end of your feeder rig. For instance, wherever the bobbin jerks upwards a couple of inches and then suddenly falls

During the brightness and heat of midday, tench can still be en-encouraged to bite even in clear water. Small hooks and the ability to hit the tiniest of twitches are the pre-requisites for consist-ent result.

A small male tench taken feeder-fishing on light tackle in bright conditions.

completely slack in a glorious drop back, this is not the fish first moving away and then turning around and swimming back towards the rod, as you might be forgiven for thinking. It is the ledger rig tightening (as the bobbin jerks up) immediately before the tension reaches too much and the feeder is pulled towards the rod, whereupon the bobbin suddenly drops. The tench has in fact been moving towards the rod from the moment it picked up the bait. These are always definite bites, because the tench is not

going to let go, and a long sweeping strike to mend the loose line nearly always connects.

Bolt-rig fishing

Moving away from feeder fishing we finally come to the shock or bolt rig. This was first devised for carp fishing, but also works well for wary tench. It is especially useful when fishing for tench which share carp fisheries, and which have been weaned on to carp baits, namely boilies and hard particles such as peanuts and black-eyed beans.

As can be seen from fig. 22, a rotten bottom is used on the bomb link, tied on to the main line with a four-turn water knot. If it snags up in weed you can continue to play

Enjoying a bout of 'twitcher hitting', John becomes cavalierish and prepares to hand out a tench instead of reaching for the net.

the tench, losing only a 1½ oz bomb. Reel line is 6 lb
(unless big tench are anticipated, in which case step up to
8 lb straight through) to a size 10 or 8 hook. If you always
sit next to the rods (within grabbing distance) this method
works best fished with a closed bale arm, although some
may consider this rather risky. After casting and dunking
the rod tip to lower the line along the bottom contours,
support the rod in two rests, pointing it at the bait. Leave a
slight bow between surface and rod tip before clipping on a
bobbin or monkey climber half way between butt ring and
reel, hanging on a 12 in drop. This scaled-down fixed-lead
rig then catches tench in the same way as it does a carp
which happens along and sucks in the boilie or particle.

As the bait is gulped back to the pharnygeal teeth for
chewing, the tench suddenly (provided the hook and
bomb links are not too long) feels the lead. It then quickly
shuts its mouth and does a runner, forgetting the bait it
was about to chew. Meanwhile, the hook is pulled down
to the lips and jerked in by the fixed lead. When the line
tightens a second later, with the tench 2 or 3 ft away and
gaining speed, the hook is really banged home. While all
this is happening (in a split second or so), the Optonic
screeches a multiple bleep, followed by the rod trying to
leave the rod rests. However, if the butt ring is jammed up
against the Optonic, the rod will stay in place. You are
then, without even having to strike, suddenly into a tench.

The bait may be side-hooked, or, if the tench are
particularly wary, sleeved on to a fine (¾ lb) hair just ½ in
long. Invariably a single bait produces a better hooking
ratio to bites, while a mini-string of tiny boilies may
induce more offers. Once the hook baits are positioned
loose feed, and an additional attractor such as hempseed,
can be scattered around with a catapult.

Good tenching

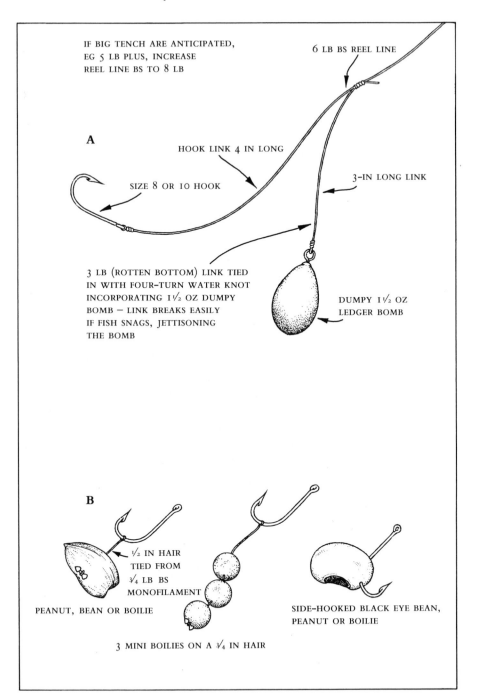

IF BIG TENCH ARE ANTICIPATED,
EG 5 LB PLUS, INCREASE
REEL LINE BS TO 8 LB

6 LB BS REEL LINE

A

HOOK LINK 4 IN LONG

3-IN LONG LINK

SIZE 8 OR 10 HOOK

3 LB (ROTTEN BOTTOM) LINK TIED
IN WITH FOUR-TURN WATER KNOT
INCORPORATING 1½ OZ DUMPY
BOMB — LINK BREAKS EASILY
IF FISH SNAGS, JETTISONING
THE BOMB

DUMPY 1½ OZ
LEDGER BOMB

B

½ IN HAIR
TIED FROM
¾ LB BS
MONOFILAMENT

PEANUT, BEAN OR BOILIE

SIDE-HOOKED BLACK EYE BEAN,
PEANUT OR BOILIE

3 MINI BOILIES ON A ¾ IN HAIR

Waiting for his free-lined whole swan mussel bait to be sucked up from beside the roots of a dense bed of white lilies, the tench fisherman has time to reflect.

INDEX